The art of innovation
How fine arts graduates contribute to innovation

Foreword

In the 21st century, the UK's economic competitiveness and social wellbeing will increasingly depend on our ability to innovate. A significant part of the innovation process revolves around 'creativity' – the ability to generate new ideas, or to restructure and redeploy old ones.

The UK has long been a leader in many of the more obvious 'creative industries': music, design, fine art, architecture and so on. Indeed, such activities can be argued to be at the heart of what the United Kingdom is about. Champions of the arts and of economic development have recently developed an alliance: they have linked this type of creativity to the type required for global competitiveness. The question is: is this link true?

NESTA has over the past year been exploring this question in a series of research reports. This time, we have been privileged to work with an outstanding team centred on the Central Saint Martins College of Art & Design in surveying and interviewing a host of fine arts graduates of the University of Arts London from the past several decades. This report gives intriguing insights into how fine arts graduates contribute to innovation in the creative industries and beyond, and what policymakers can do to support their contribution. We plan to put these insights to good use in some of NESTA's practical experiments over the next few years.

As always, we thank you for your interest and in advance for your contribution to this debate.

Jonathan Kestenbaum
CEO, NESTA

September, 2008

NESTA is the National Endowment for Science, Technology and the Arts.

Our aim is to transform the UK's capacity for innovation. We invest in early-stage companies, inform innovation policy and encourage a culture that helps innovation to flourish.

Executive summary

1. See Appendix 2 for full details.

The art of innovation is an inquiry into how fine arts graduates contribute to innovation through their working lives
The art of innovation is the result of a nine-month study into the working lives of fine arts graduates and the ways in which they contribute to innovation, both within the arts and in the wider economy.

The research is based on a cohort study of fine arts students who have graduated since the 1950s from the University of the Arts in London (and its constituent colleges). The sample includes those who have studied painting, sculpture, fine art photography, fine art, film and video or combined arts as undergraduates or postgraduates. It consists of an online survey completed by over 500 members of the University of the Arts London (UAL) alumni association and 40 face-to-face work biography interviews.

We use a combination of survey and interview techniques
By using a survey followed by interviews, we have been able to identify patterns and regularities through the survey and to look for potential causal processes through the work biography interviews. This two-pronged approach has enabled us to explore what innovation processes look like *in situ* rather than testing an *a priori* model. Our approach thus combines quantitative and qualitative data, and our intention is to try and understand these debates from the point of view of fine arts graduates themselves. We want to see how artists understand innovation and how that

understanding shapes the way they work, both as fine artists and in other sectors.

The majority of our survey respondents and interviewees work in the cultural and creative industries in their primary occupations
Although our focus is on fine arts graduates, not artists overall, just over 40 per cent of our questionnaire sample say that they work primarily in the arts and cultural industries, with a further 6 per cent working in publishing and media. With another 11 per cent in design, crafts and new media, a total of almost 60 per cent of our graduates work in the wider cultural and creative industries; a further 20 per cent or so work in education, 4 per cent in health care and the remainder in 'other sectors'.[1]

This is consistent with the literature which suggests that those trained in the arts will endeavour to remain in them throughout their career (Throsby and Hollister, 2003; Aston, 1999; Blackwell and Harvey, 1999); it also suggests that many of our graduates are indeed successful in remaining within them.

The numbers of fine arts graduates working in the cultural industries is increasing
Indeed, if we look at our respondents by decade of graduation, it appears that increasing numbers of fine arts graduates work in the arts and cultural industries – some 65 per cent of 1990s graduates, for example, say they work primarily in these sectors. The 'arts and cultural industries' are of course a much bigger sector than the 'fine arts', but there

seems to be a clear preference for cultural work – and a supply of jobs to satisfy this demand.

There are three main ways in which artistic labour is linked into innovation

Beyond the expansion of the cultural and creative sectors themselves, however, the literature suggests at least three ways in which artistic labour is absorbed into the wider economy and linked into processes of innovation.

1. They have attitudes and skills that are conducive to innovation

Lester and Piore (2004) suggest that innovation depends on two processes: analysis and interpretation. Analysis is essentially rational decision-making, familiar from the processes of science and technology. It works best when the alternative outcomes are well understood and can be clearly defined. Interpretation, on the other hand, is a process of mutual understanding arrived at through exploratory conversations with a variety of collaborators. As Lester and Piore argue (2004:6): "interpretive processes are more appropriate when the possible outcomes are unknown – when the task is to create those outcomes". It thus requires a willingness to try new things, tolerance of ambiguity and has a clear need for 'brokers' or people who can interpret across disciplinary boundaries.

In this study, when describing how processes of innovation take place in their own work fine arts graduates often describe a process which is akin to this notion of interpretive innovation. Although the term 'innovation' is itself rarely used, respondents often speak of a desire for change or novelty in their own work, allied to a dislike of repetition. In many cases, they don't know how work will turn out when they start, or its outcome emerges gradually. This is also something that respondents describe carrying over into other forms of work and cross-disciplinary collaborations.

a. Many fine arts graduates describe themselves as brokers across disciplines
The process of innovation that is described is generally social – close links to social and professional networks open up new opportunities, and the process of creating or pursuing new opportunities often crosses disciplinary boundaries. In crossing these boundaries, interviewees often describe their role as one of brokering between disciplinary

specialities, "taking the model of X and applying it to Y", as one interviewee puts it.

b. They demonstrate the traits of lifelong learners, including frequent use of informal and formal training throughout their working lives
What we might call the skills or attributes of innovators appear highly developed in this workforce, particularly the degree to which they display the habits of lifelong learners (Seltzer and Bentley, 1999). Overall, almost 44 per cent of survey respondents have received some formal training after fine arts study and almost 80 per cent have participated in informal learning.

This participation in lifelong learning is not just confined to those who work in the arts and cultural sectors. It seems to be a characteristic of fine arts graduates and is arguably one which is learned or developed during art school education, where there is a significant emphasis on unstructured time spent in the studio, and learning is essentially a process of discovery, aided, but not directed, by experts.

c. They single out their own consumption of art as a stimulus for their own work
Another aspect of interpretive innovation that Lester and Piore (2004) observe is closeness to consumers, particularly in cultural sectors like the fashion industry. What is less often commented upon, but is nonetheless important for our respondents, is the artist's own role as a consumer. Respondents often stress the importance of immersion in the work of other artists when describing their art school education; this is also described as a factor in the 'stickiness' of London as an art world hub. This does not exclude traditional consumers or audiences, but it does highlight the importance of the personal consumption of culture in its further production.

2. Artistic labour impacts on innovation in the way that it is organised – project work and portfolio working are the norm

The way artistic labour is organised makes artists arguably a prototype not just for work organisation, but for innovation in the rest of the economy. As Ruth Towse argues (2001), typical features of artistic labour markets – casualisation, self-employment, the project-based company – are becoming more widespread in the economy as a whole.

From an innovation perspective, the importance of this form of work organisation is perhaps less what it tells us about the labour market and more what it tells us about the crossover and cross-fertilisation of people and ideas across the arts, and between the arts and non-arts worlds.

a. There are very high rates of multi-jobbing in cultural and non-cultural sectors

Consistent with other such surveys (Throsby and Hollister, 2003), nearly 40 per cent of survey respondents currently hold a second job. This percentage varies little by decade of graduation. Of those 40 per cent, around three in five hold a second job outside the arts and cultural industries, primarily in education, health care and other service sectors.

b. 'Crossover' takes place throughout artists' working lives

While the survey allows us to see a snapshot of an already complicated picture, the interviews enable us to look over people's entire careers, where we see that very few people are likely only to have worked in the arts or in the 'rest of the economy'. We could indeed argue that such 'crossover' happens continually throughout many artists' lives.

The assumption of much of the literature, influenced by cultural economist David Throsby, is that artists use money earned from other work to supplement their meagre income from artistic work or to buy time for their practice. There is certainly much evidence for this in both our questionnaire responses and the interviews.

c. Financial reasons force many artists to seek employment in non-cultural sectors

We ask people in our survey why they decide to seek employment outside the arts. The response rate is low, as most of our respondents consider themselves to be artists, but for those who do reply, the 'need for regular work and income' sums up just over a third of responses. It is clear from both survey and interviews that financial reasons are a factor in taking up other careers.

d. But crossover also brings opportunities for learning new skills

What becomes clearer through the interviews, however, is that many respondents gain valuable skills, ideas and contacts both from their artistic activities and their other work. This is not to gloss over the economic reality of a labour market which often necessitates multiple job-holding and where unpaid work is common; but it does suggest that even if financial issues drive crossover, it is not the only reason, and the benefits can extend beyond supplementary income.

This multi-jobbing also highlights the weaknesses of strong occupational categorisations within these sectors which make it difficult to quantify the degree of crossover between the fine arts and other parts of the economy. More importantly, it suggests that instead of focussing on 'work in the rest of the economy' as being the way in which fine arts graduates are linked into innovation, we need to focus on this constant cross-fertilisation.

3. Artistic labour impacts on innovation through the widespread 'culturalisation' of activities

Culture is becoming a more important part of all production (Lash and Urry, 1993), which accounts for the absorption of increased amounts of artistic labour.

In this 'culturisation' thesis, not only are traditional 'cultural products' – books, music, films – increasing in number, but cultural ideas and images are also increasingly a part of non-cultural products and services from retail environments to running shoes. In this way, cultural labour provides content that requires 'artistic creativity' as a knowledge-based and labour-intensive input into a whole variety of goods and services.

a. But fine arts graduates remain keen to stress the distinction between cultural and non-cultural pursuits

However, while fine arts graduates work across both cultural and non-cultural occupations, they continue to distinguish between the two in a way that suggests that they retain a meaningful notion of separate cultural sectors.

As might be expected from those trained in the fine arts, respondents often use the term 'creativity' when describing their work. But their use of this term differs from that favoured by policymakers. Creativity, when it is used, generally describes a process, not a product. Respondents are thus more likely to talk about 'being creative' in their approach to work, rather than as producing a 'creative output'. So, because terms like the 'creative industries' are rarely used by this group, such a discourse risks underplaying artists as a core component of cultural production.

b. However, they don't see creativity as the exclusive preserve of the arts
Our interviewees do not regard creativity as synonymous with culture or the arts. Both cultural and external work can be creative or formulaic. Work in other parts of the economy is not necessarily seen as being 'less creative'.

The distinction between cultural products and non-cultural products is however still clear in the minds our respondents. When someone says, "I think in itself, it isn't innovation, it's just art work", or defines professional art work as, "something that serves no purpose", it is clear that the distinction between symbolic and utilitarian production still has relevance for this group.

c. So, policies to support the wider innovation benefits of the fine arts must recognise the complex mechanisms by which crossover takes place
Emerging policies to support the benefits that fine artists bring to innovation in the wider economy need to recognise these different understandings of culture and creativity, the multi-dimensional nature of crossover and the distinct mechanisms through which fine artists contribute to innovation.

Acknowledgements

We would like to thank the following interviewees for giving up their time and sharing their experiences:

Stephen Amor	Colin Grigg	Lisha Aquino Rooney
Lea Anderson	David Gryn	Caroline Salmon
Jessica Baum	Caitlin Heffernan	Anne-Marie Sapalska
Caspar Below	Susanna Heron	Polly Segal
Marc Brzezicki	Jean Hill	Azadi Sheridan
Philip Butler	Flip Jelly	Lisette Stalbow
Kezia Cantwell-Wright	Debbie Lawson	Shubha Talapia
Elena Cologni	Josie McCoy	Steven Thomas
Françoise Dupré	Tim Molloy	Becky Tunstall
Rebecca Foster	Belle Mundy	Catherine Wake
Vivian Fuller	Harriet Murray	Celia Washington
Noel Hawks	Douglas Nicolson	Anna Binns Williams
Rachel Garfield	Tamarin Norwood	
Charles Garrad	Nicholas Romeril	

We would also like to thanks members of the Steering Committee for comments and advice:

Dani Salvadori (Central Saint Martins, University of the Arts London)

Anne Bamford (Wimbledon College of Art, University of the Arts London)

Emily Keaney (Arts Council England)

Hasan Bakhshi (NESTA)

Martin Woolley (Central Saint Martins, University of the Arts London)

Tom Campbell (London Development Agency)

David Whitaker (University of the Arts London)

Stephen Beddoe (Artquest, University of the Arts London)

Kirsty Leith (DCMS)

This research and report was managed for NESTA by Hasan Bakhshi. Dani Salvadori managed the project at Central Saint Martins Innovation with the help of the University of the Arts London Alumni Association.

Contents

Part 1: Introduction

We examine how the work practices
of successive generations of fine arts
graduates have impacted on innovation

The aim of this project is to investigate the
work practices of fine arts graduates and their
impact on innovation. Uniquely, for such a
study, we look at long-term changes: by using
a 50-year period, we also examine the extent
to which those changes provide a deeper
understanding of the way fine artists and their
skills have been transferred into the wider
society and economy, and the role that this
process plays in stimulating innovation.

The research is based on a cohort study of
individuals who have graduated with fine
arts qualifications since the 1950s from the
University of Arts London

The research is based on a cohort study of
individuals who have graduated with fine
arts qualifications since the 1950s from the
University of the Arts in London (and its
constituent colleges).[2] The University of the
Arts London (UAL, previously known as the
London Institute) was awarded university
status in 2004. It has six constituent colleges:
Camberwell College of Arts, Central Saint
Martins College of Art and Design, Chelsea
College of Art and Design, London College of
Communication, London College of Fashion,
and Wimbledon College of Art.

As the largest university for art, design,
fashion, communication and the performing
arts in Europe, it has approximately 28,000
students. As such it is an exemplar institution, a
leader in its field. Methodologically, this means
that we are not seeking to generalise our
findings; however, our research does provide a
sharp and rich insight into processes that are
found – to a greater or lesser extent – in all arts
practice.

For this project, we define as artists those who
pursue an artistic practice, paid or unpaid,
full or part time. As we are studying fine arts
graduates, not artists, this definition is less
important to us than to some other studies
(Throsby and Hollister, 2003), which look solely
at artists in the professional sense. Yet while we
are focusing on fine arts graduates – who may
be working in very different fields and may not
practise any art form – the majority of those
we sample do define themselves as 'artists'. We
have accepted this self-definition.

We use both quantitative survey techniques
and qualitative interview methods

This report is part of a series of projects
(Stoneman, 2007, 2008; Miles and Green,
2008; Bakhshi, McVittie and Simmie, 2008;
Higgs, Cunningham and Bakhshi, 2008)
commissioned by NESTA into the role of the
arts and creative sectors in innovation. Much
of this work is quantitative, for example using
input-output accounts to examine the links
between the creative sectors and other parts of
the economy, or using census and labour force
data to track how creative occupations are
embedded in the rest of the economy.

Our approach combines quantitative and
qualitative data, using an online survey
followed by a series of career biography
interviews. Our intention is to try to understand
these debates from the point of view of fine
arts graduates themselves. We want to see how
artists understand innovation and how that
understanding shapes the way they work, both
as fine artists and when they are working in
other sectors.

2. The sample includes
those who have studied
painting, sculpture, fine art
photography, fine art, film
and video or combined arts.

A distinguishing characteristic of our approach is that we draw out fine arts graduates' own notions of innovation and relate those back to concepts used by policymakers

For a piece of research in innovation we deliberately begin with a critical stance. We adopted this critical stance to avoid prior expectations and a simple 'read across' from the notion of innovation in engineering and science. A key aim is to develop a notion of innovation from the participants and then to compare and contrast this with the commonly accepted notions which populate the policy and wider academic literature. This, we argue, is a major contribution of this study: an appreciation of the 'varieties of innovation' and some insight into what innovation means to the artist.

We focus on three possible mechanisms by which artistic labour may impact on innovation in the economy

Given a 60 per cent increase in the number of art and design graduates in the UK economy in the last decade, our study also investigates mechanisms that could account for their increased absorption into the economy.

3. A longer literature review is included in Oakley and Sperry (2008).

The first is that fine arts graduates have the attitudes and skills that are needed for innovation

The first is the notion advanced by Lester and Piore (2004) in their book, *Innovation: The Missing Dimension*, that artists are particularly important in 'third generation innovation' due to their particular training, their disposition towards critical thinking and their close understanding of consumer needs. Harnessing these innovative tendencies requires a willingness to try new things, a tolerance of ambiguity and 'brokers' who can interpret across disciplinary boundaries.

The second is that the way artistic labour is organised is a prototype for innovation

The second hypothesis is that it is the way artistic labour is organised through networks rather than firms – as well as the less desirable aspects of cultural work, such as that which is unpaid – that makes it a prototype not just for work organisation, but for innovation in the rest of the economy. This mode of work organisation also explains how fine artists interact with the rest of the economy – through a form of networked labour that ensures constant crossover between the arts and the wider world.

The third mechanism is that cultural ideas are increasingly embedded in non-cultural goods and services

The final hypothesis, the 'culturisation' thesis, is that cultural ideas and images are an increasingly important part of non-cultural products and services from retail environments to running shoes. In this way, cultural labour provides content that requires 'artistic creativity' as a knowledge-based and labour-intensive input into a whole variety of goods and services.

The structure of the report is as follows:

- Part 2 outlines the relevant literatures that form the background to the study.[3]

- Part 3 outlines the research methodology.

- Part 4 presents the primary research evidence, from both the survey and interviews.

- Part 5 outlines the relevant issues for policymakers that arise from the research.

- Part 6 presents the summary and conclusions.

Given the scope of the study, much of the supporting material can be found in the Appendices. Appendix 1 features a longer description of the research methodology, while Appendices 2, 3 and 4 give more details on the survey and interview evidence.

Part 2: Artists and innovation

2.1 Introduction

This study looks at how artistically trained labour contributes to innovation
The purpose of this section is to set the wider context in which this study is taking place, and to help us outline our key hypotheses.

While innovation is widely acknowledged as a factor in economic growth, the relationship between creativity and innovation is more vexed; though – intriguingly for the current research – some recent thinking suggests that innovation may be more a cultural activity than a science (Lester and Piore, 2004). So, we might learn a lot about innovation from artistic work.

We focus on the absorption and use of artistically trained labour as a way of examining these phenomena. Our understanding of training goes beyond functional skills; it includes notions such as taste, attitude and disposition (Bourdieu, 1984).

2.2 So how do the arts contribute to innovation?

Attempts to understand the links between the arts and innovation are hampered by definitional challenges
Systematic attempts to understand links between culture, the creative industries and the wider economy are very much in the early stages (see Bakhshi, McVittie and Simmie, 2008, for one approach). One difficulty with work in this field is its imprecise and often slippery terminology. While 'culture' is itself widely acknowledged to be a problematic term (Williams, 1976), 'creativity' is no more straightforward, as it sounds evaluative rather than descriptive when applied to particular economic sectors. Thus the question, 'but aren't other industries creative as well?', has always dogged the creative industries debate.

The *Cox Review* (HM Treasury, 2005) defines creativity as the generation of new ideas. Cox doesn't claim that culture and the arts are the only source of these 'new ideas'. But the Review suggests a privileged role for design, which is defined as the link between creativity (the generation of new ideas) and innovation (the successful exploitation of those ideas).

Such a definition simply raises another question – what counts as 'new'? Notions such as newness, innovation or creativity depend on situation, occasion and context. The innovator's skill, as Latour (1988) notes in his study of pasteurisation, is successfully to extend a specific innovative context to the wider population. So, education is a common framework within which classical art resonates and draws value. Or, more parochially, the critical debates about a piece of music both prime and prepare a new audience.

We focus on three main ways that artistic labour may impact on innovation
There are at least three ways in which artistic labour might be linked into the process of innovation. These are discussed below.

2.3 The culture of innovation – the relevance of 'artistic' skills

Artists may have experimental skills and attitudes which are seen as important for innovation

Lester and Piore (2004) argue that artists are important in 'third generation innovation' due to their particular training, their disposal towards critical thinking, and their close understanding of consumer needs. "The capacity to experiment and the habits of thought that allow us to make sense of radically ambiguous situations and move forward in the face of uncertainty" are associated with artistic creativity, and are important for innovation, particularly where science and technology are not on their own drivers.

Their preferred work methods are interpretive as opposed to analytical

Lester and Piore suggest that innovation depends on two processes: analysis and interpretation. While analysis is essentially rational decision-making, familiar from science and technology, it works best when the alternative outcomes are well understood and can be clearly defined. Interpretation, on the other hand, is a process of mutual understanding arrived at through exploratory conversations with a variety of collaborators. It is less about solving clearly defined problems than initiating and guiding conversations. Others find similar processes to be important in design, with Verganti (2003) arguing that "design is the brokering of languages".

Artists work with tacit knowledge

Ikujoro Nonaka and Hirotake Takeuchi have looked at the innovation process in Japanese manufacturing industry, though their findings have a wider resonance. According to Nonaka, making personal or tacit knowledge available to others is the central activity of the 'knowledge-creating company'. But this process of converting tacit knowledge into explicit or codified knowledge resembles creative practice rather than an analytical approach, where alternatives are well understood and clearly defined.

> "First by linking contradictory things and ideas through metaphor; then by resolving these contradictions through analogy; and finally, by crystallizing the created concepts and embodying them in a model, which makes the knowledge available to the rest of the company." (Nonaka, 1991:101)

Artists arguably have a high tolerance for uncertainty and ambiguity

Similarly, attitudes to uncertainty (Bryce *et al.* 2004) and tolerance of ambiguity appear to be essential to the interpretive mode of innovation, whereas a more analytical approach would proceed by reducing ambiguity and uncertainty. Lester and Piore (2004) go so far as to claim that "ambiguity is the critical resource out of which new ideas emerge". It is this ambiguity that makes "the conversation worth having" rather than the actual exchange of information. If the conversation is narrowed or closed off too soon, and the ambiguity eliminated, potential innovations can be lost.

As consumers of art, many artists are well-placed to satisfy consumer needs

Lester and Piore (2004) observe the close connections between consumers and producers in the fashion industry. Traditional analytical innovation suggests that understanding the customer's needs is a pre-requisite to developing suitable products or services. But few fashion items respond to need: they tend to be positional or symbolic goods. Lester and Piore show how, in understanding clothing only partly as a functional utility, and in their close observation of how clothes are interpreted and customised, fashion companies seem closer to consumer attitudes than other firms.

Unlike pharmaceuticals, where the development of a new drug requires a highly detailed formal knowledge base, systematic experimentation and extensive clinical trials, the cultural industries arguably rely on a more informal knowledge base, a 'feel' for what people might want, partly based on the creators' own experience as a consumer.[4] Otherwise expressed, this 'feel' is the ability to navigate taste and fashion: the success or failure of which is the difference between winning and losing in a high stakes (cultural) economy.

2.4 Artists as workers – the organisation of cultural labour markets

The organisation of artistic labour may also influence innovation

The attitudes of artistic workers and the way artistic labour is organised through networks rather than firms – as well as the less desirable aspects such as unpaid cultural work – make them a prototype not just for work organisation, but for innovation in the rest of the economy.

Cultural production typically occurs in flexible networks and temporary, project-based collaborations

4. This does not mean of course that a formal knowledge base and systematic experimentation play no role in the cultural industries.

The creation of new cultural products usually occurs in flexible networks and temporary, project-based collaborations (Caves, 2000); creative labour markets are also extremely flexible and volatile (Benhamou, 2002). Most cultural product life-cycles tend to be short, and creative industries exhibit intensive user-producer interaction. The importance of entrepreneurship in these sectors (Leadbeater and Oakley, 1999) and the impact of rapid technological change on the industrial structure of sub-sectors such as the music industry (Hesmondhalgh, 2002) have attracted both academic and policymakers' attention.

Such features are becoming more widespread in the economy as a whole

As Ruth Towse argues (2001), typical features of artistic labour markets – casualisation, self-employment, the project-based company – are becoming more widespread in the economy as a whole.

Artistic labour markets also appear to display some marked differences from traditional labour markets: in particular, they do not conform to human capital models where workers' investment in training and learning are expected to produce higher earnings (Towse, 2001). Throsby (1992) suggests that earnings for artists do not necessarily rise in line with formal training, nor with years of experience; 'experienced' cultural producers do not necessarily earn more than their younger counterparts.

Intrinsic motivation to be artists means that labour markets don't operate along traditional lines

The willingness of people to undertake artistic education continually produces an 'oversupply' of artists, leading to apparently lower earnings than similarly-qualified professionals (Towse, 1995; Menger 1999). People continue to want to enter cultural labour markets, as we shall see, for intrinsic rewards and job satisfaction or simply because they believe they may be among the minority that 'makes it' (McRobbie, 2002).

This can make artists attractive workers for employers

This willingness to work for low (or no) pay in relatively insecure conditions underlies what some commentators see as the attractiveness of cultural workers to employers in other parts of the economy. As Andrew Ross (2003) comments, in his study of artists-turned-new-media-workers, *No Collar*, "artists (in the broad

sense of the term) come with training in what could be called sacrificial labor".

This, he argues, makes them 'predisposed' to accept non-monetary rewards such as the gratification of practising their art. They are therefore valued by employers who seek long hours, ideas and emotional commitment from their workforce. For Ross's 'net slaves', "it was cool to be addicted to overwork. But, as Ross himself notes, this may have as much to do with artistic traditions of self-exploitation as it does with the requirements of their bosses. The 'mentality' of artists has simply become too valuable to be left to artists alone; it is instead increasingly in demand in the contemporary knowledge and service sectors.

2.5 Culture is everywhere

A final channel through which artistic labour can affect innovation is through the increasingly widespread use of cultural symbols

The argument that culture is becoming a more important part of all production is increasingly familiar (Lash and Urry, 1993). Most cars will get one from A to B. The difference between a Mercedes and a less expensive model is less about utility and more about intangible aspects, such as 'style'; these are often the product of cultural labour.

Others argue that cultural objects themselves proliferate in a variety of forms:

> "As information, as communications, as branded products, as media products, as transport and leisure services, cultural entities are no longer the exception: they are the rule." (Lash and Urry, 2007)

In this 'culturisation' thesis, cultural products are no longer primarily symbolic, but have become 'things,' when:

> "for example movies become computer games; when brands become brand environments, taking over airport terminal space and restructuring department stores, road billboards and city centres; when cartoon characters become collectibles and costumes; when music is played in lifts, part of a mobile soundscape". (Lash and Urry, 2007)

Artistic creativity becomes a knowledge-based input into a variety of goods and services

So, not only are traditional 'cultural products' – books, music, films – increasing in number, but cultural ideas and images are also increasingly a part of non-cultural products and services from retail environments to running shoes. In this way, cultural labour provides content that requires 'artistic creativity' as a knowledge-based and labour-intensive input into a whole variety of goods. As Menger (1999) points out, these goods can also include public goods, such as local economic development or urban regeneration, which have increasingly required a cultural 'input' into iconic buildings, public art or gallery content.

The artist's critical disposition may itself be seen as a key function in society

A separate, subtler and less quantifiable, argument is that, as Ruth Towse (2001) puts it, "the Beatles didn't just create pop music; they played a leading role in a cultural, social, political and economic revolution".

In this argument, what Boltanski and Chiapello (2005) call the 'artistic critique' – the bohemian spirit derived from 19th century attacks on bourgeois conformity and hierarchy – is the artist's real contribution to contemporary society.

Some argue that this critique may have lost force as an anti-capitalist argument (Boltanski and Chiapello, 2005; Heath and Potter, 2005). The 'bohemian' lifestyle, celebrated by Richard Florida (2002) and others, has itself become a source of new goods and services.

In this version of Bohemia, the desire to 'stand out from the crowd' or express one's individuality is often articulated through consumer purchases. As in Apple's iconic '1984' advertisement for personal computers, the 'rebel' individual is the one who rejects the 'big' brands (at the time symbolised by IBM) in favour of another product; in the process, they help to turn the 'rebel product' into a big brand. As Heath and Potter (2005) argue, in this way:

> "the critique of mass society has been one of the most powerful forces driving consumerism for the past forty years".

Whatever accounts for the growth in differentiated consumer products, we are clearly a long way from the 'any colour, as long as it is black' world of Fordist production. What is less clear is the role of artists themselves in the culturisation thesis and the extent to which it has changed the demand for their labour.

2.6 The geography of the cultural industries

There is a large literature on the geography of the cultural industries (e.g. Scott, 2000; Pratt, 2002; Markusen and King, 2003; Mommaas, 2004). Our interest is primarily in what the literature tells us about the geographical determinants of cultural innovation, particularly the relationship between innovation outcomes and the local interaction between artists and other workers.

Recent economic geography (Knudsen, Florida and Stolarick, forthcoming) has focused on the inter-related concepts of proximity, face-to-face interaction and knowledge spillovers; in this respect, the cultural sectors exemplify many of the factors that promote growth in a knowledge-based economy.

Cultural workers remain bound in place, even in the digital world

The ability of expensive, inner-city neighbourhoods to retain their productive employment in the cultural industries puzzles many, who are perplexed by why creative and cultural workers remain bound to place, as distance working becomes technically easier. But, as much recent research has demonstrated (Pratt, 2005a and b; Neff, 2005; Storper and Venables, 2004), even new digital technology firms have a tendency to co-locate, generally in major cities, and often within the same neighbourhood or building.

The explanations are often mutually reinforcing. Pratt's (2005b) study of the London film industry has examined the importance of personal communication, particularly at the early developmental stage of projects, when uncertainty is high and negotiations are complex. This constant exchange of information, together with informal exchanges such as rumour and industry gossip, are the 'untraded inter-dependences' crucial to individuals' and firms' ability to innovate in fast-changing markets.

As Athey et al. (2007) point out in their discussion of London's fashion industry, the city's fashion designers are aided not only by the critical mass of people and businesses working in their own area, but by access to nearby specialist media and the related sub-cultures of design, music and the visual arts.

In some cultural sectors, such as the media, the structure of the sector – a few large players, surrounded by much smaller companies and a large pool of freelance labour – means that information exchange often happens beyond the boundaries of the firm. This increases the importance of close, often social settings.

Social ties play an important role in facilitating knowledge exchange

Neff's work on digital media in New York's Silicon Alley (Neff, 2005; Pratt 2000, 2002) demonstrates the importance not only of social ties, but of places where these social ties could be formed. Thus the 'night time economy' of Lower Manhattan – its parties, bars, clubs and informal gatherings – plays a crucial part in enabling exchange between the large number of small new media firms in the city (Currid, 2007).

The venues for these meetings can also be invested with 'symbolic capital': the association of warehouse spaces with artists, or former industrial areas with creativity, gives them a particular value (albeit sometimes a problematic one, where gentrification is perceived to have driven out artists or other low-paid groups).

A city's leisure infrastructure also offers artists opportunities for multiple job-holding

A less recognised but no less important aspect of the city's leisure infrastructure is the opportunity it offers for multiple job-holding to artists who are unable to make a living income from artistic work alone. In his ethnography of the Wicker Park area of Chicago, Richard Lloyd (2006) shows how many young creatives subsidised their unpaid artistic work through a variety of service sector jobs particularly in bars and restaurants. He argues that the 'performative' nature of cultural work often serves workers well in service industries which require "the mastery of hip social codes".

The existence of a large service sector and a buoyant consumer economy to sustain it, characteristic of urban environments, is therefore part of the mix that enables the cultural sectors to function. These factors are often mutually dependent, reliant on the combination of access to labour pools, tacit information, 'the right address' and the cultural consumption preferences of workers.

2.7 Networks and work organisation

Networks allow the sharing of ideas and tacit knowledge between artists

This need for proximity and the importance of personal contact in cultural work also helps to explain the importance of the network, both as an organisational form for creative and cultural firms, and for groups of individuals such as artists.

The supportive environment and local, tacit knowledge are vital in helping with everything from finance to premises or staff. At the same time, the transfer of ideas and skills takes place, with workers often engaged in multiple and overlapping projects. This complex form of labour pooling enables people to develop reputations and pedigree, vital in a field with so many formally-qualified workers (Pratt, 2006).

But the exclusivity associated with networks can pose challenges for attempts to increase diversity

From the outside, the networking involved in cultural activities often seems incestuous and exclusive. It also poses a problem for public policymakers keen to open the cultural sectors up to a more diverse range of producers (Oakley, 2006; Andari et al., 2007). There is often a tension between the trust needed in the risky, experimental stages of creation and the need to be sufficiently porous to allow new talent into the system (Bilton, 2007).

2.8 Art and design in UK higher education

There has been a marked increase in the numbers of students with higher education arts qualifications

The expansion of higher education in the UK is well documented. The annual Students and Qualifiers Data published by the Higher Education Statistics Agency (HESA) for 2005/06, reveals more than 156,000 students in creative arts and design, an increase of over 60 per cent in the past decade. Looking specifically at the figures for fine arts programmes, there were just under 40,000 students in 2005/6 (HESA, 2005).

Formal art and design education in the UK has a much shorter history than in some other European countries, such as Italy or France. Yet art and design was also the first area of education to receive public funding. Design education was funded by Parliament in 1837 to improve the knowledge of art and design principles in the manufacturing sector, in order to raise competitiveness against European exports after the passing of free trade agreements (Bird, 2000).

The history of arts education in the UK has been one of a gradual increase in credentialisation

The subsequent story of arts education in the UK is one of a gradual and sometimes contentious move towards credentialisation (Frith and Horne, 1987; Bracewell, 2007). The National Diploma in Design (NDD), introduced in 1946, was built around specialist courses. They were taught at local arts schools, but examined centrally.

The Coldstream Report elevated the status of many fine arts qualifications to degree level

The Coldstream Report on Fine Art Teaching (Ministry of Education, 1960), saw NDDs replaced by Diplomas in Art and Design (Dip. ADs). The Diplomas had the status of university degrees. More significantly, they demanded revised entry qualifications of five 'O' Levels, of which at least three should be in 'acceptable' academic subjects, and the minimum entry age was raised to 18 years.

This higher entry age meant that most, if not all, students were now expected to complete a foundation year, often at their own local art college. The foundation was intended to 'sort' or even weed out students between school and higher education. But, as our interviews show, many respondents regard foundation, with its wealth of possibilities, as the most important element of their art school education.

These changes led to what one commentator describes as the "slaughter of arts and design education" (MacDonald, 2005), with most art colleges failing to meet the criteria for offering the Dip. AD course (Frith and Horne, 1987).

Coldstream also had major implications for the syllabus and method of art school teaching

Equally contentiously, the Coldstream Report mandated a component of historical and contextual study in fine arts degrees, which some saw as an attack on the practice-based nature of art education (MacDonald, 2005). However, it would be difficult to argue that the Coldstream changes led to an abandonment of practice in favour of essay-

writing; Coldstream also supported what has been called the "open model" (Mulvey, 2006) of fine arts teaching based on the concept of time for studio practice. This system, with its focus on unstructured time in the studio, still continues, though some of our recent interviewees suggest that the more recent massive expansion of higher education may have affected the quality of this experience.

2.9 Studies of artists' employment and careers

A series of research projects into the careers of art and design graduates was launched at the Birmingham Institute of Art and Design (BIAD) in 1996.

Aston (1999) focused on two patterns in particular: graduates' propensity to remain in art and design, and the extent to which they became involved with teaching.

Ambitions and Destinations (Aston, 1999) provides the springboard for further research into the careers of art and design graduates. Blackwell and Harvey (1999) argue that, by the mid-90s, UK employers were more concerned that graduates possess a core set of interactive and personal skills and attitudes than about the subject of their degree. The report challenges the stereotype of unemployed or unemployable arts graduates. The findings also suggest that most art and design graduates work in the art and design field after graduating; just 20 per cent of respondents undertake work unrelated to art and design and fewer than 5 per cent are unemployed.

Researchers have previously noted that fine arts graduates often experience a difficult 'first year' out of art school

Blackwell and Harvey note that art and design (and especially fine arts) graduates often experience a difficult 'first year' after graduation as they struggle to make contacts, organise a portfolio, and negotiate (often multiple) work contracts. They also echo the high rate of self-employment established by previous studies.

Don't Give Up Your Day Job: An Economic Study of Professional Artists in Australia (Throsby and Hollister, 2003) seeks to view artists' working lives alongside broad trends in the political, social, and cultural environments. The study is notable for its methods of selecting artists: 'practising professional artists' are self-defined and must have been artistically active in the previous three to five years. They are not, however, required to have earned income from this practice.

The 'big break' for many artists is often seen to be the first solo show or publication, rather than completion of their degree

Established practice is not defined by income, but rather by the artist's self-defined "commitment" and "achievement" (Throsby and Hollister, 2003), in a break with traditional labour market analysis. The moment of establishment or "big break" is most often identified as the first solo show or publication (42 per cent); only 6 per cent see it as the completion of training.

The literature suggests that multi-jobbing among artists is common

The majority of Throsby and Hollister's respondents had held more than one job at any one time. When the preferred working patterns of visual artists are considered, 41 per cent report spending less than 100 per cent of their working time on arts work; of those, 73 per cent would like to spend more time at arts work. The overwhelming barrier preventing artists from spending time at work is "insufficient income from that work"; other significant barriers are "work in occupation not available" and "domestic responsibilities or childcare".

Crossover: How Artists Build Careers across Commercial, Nonprofits and Community Work (Markusen *et al.* 2006) provides a starting point for our own survey. Markusen *et al.* outline the three spheres in which they see artists primarily working:

1. The commercial sector, driven by for-profit organisations that employ artists; this sector includes self-employed artists who market by themselves.

2. The not-for-profit sector, commissioned and/or largely supported by the public sector or not-for-profit organisations (including museums and not-for-profit foundation grants). This is roughly equivalent to the European notion of a public sector.

3. The community sector, in which artistic practice is often unpaid "but pursued for cultural, political and aesthetic reasons" by "informal" forums or organisations, outside

the spheres of both the commercial art market(s) and not-for-profits.

Crossover gives artists multiple earning and non-earning opportunities to develop their work

Many artists surveyed by *Crossover* practise in all three sectors, which, it argues, leads to different types of artistic development. Working in the commercial sector provides an 'understanding of artistic and professional conventions', broader visibility and networking opportunities that positively impact on practice and deliver higher rates of return. The not-for-profit sector is perceived to contribute to artistic development in terms of aesthetic and emotional satisfaction, and provides opportunities for explorative and collaborative practice. Working in the community sector leads artists to develop a positive community life, a stronger cultural identity and support for integrated social and political activism.

Cross-subsidy of artistic work by paid employment in other sectors is not unusual

Crossover unsurprisingly finds that artists make more money working in the commercial sector for the time spent there; working in the not-for-profit sector pays less money for more time; and the same is true to an even greater degree for the community sector. The survey also finds that artists cross-subsidise work in the not-for-profit and community sectors with money earned from more lucrative commercial work.

Much of the existing research illuminates the patterns of artistic careers, their motivations and their working lives (Frey, 1997; Blackwell and Harvey, 1999; Rengers and Madden, 2000). But the fine arts are generally viewed as a self-contained world and the literature is rarely linked explicitly to that on the broader culture and creative sectors, let alone innovation.

An exception is the relatively limited work on those with art school training, and their influence on other areas of the economy, notably popular culture. Such work includes Frith and Horne's book on art school graduates and pop music (Frith and Horne, 1987) and Michael Bracewell's recent book (Bracewell, 2007), which offers a detailed exploration of the role of art school education in producing a vibrant UK popular music scene in the 1970s and 1980s.

Part 3: Research methodology

This study employs both quantitative survey and qualitative interview techniques
This study combines a primarily quantitative survey with intensive qualitative methods.[5] It consists of an online survey completed by over 500 members of the University of the Arts London (UAL) alumni association,[6] a follow-up survey, posted on various artist websites, and 40 face-to-face work biography interviews.

The advantage of this approach is that we can identify patterns and regularities through the quantitative data and look for potential causal processes through the qualitative analysis. This two-pronged approach enables us to explore what innovation processes looks like *in situ* rather than testing an *a priori* model.

The survey responses yield data on artists' working lives for over 500 fine arts graduates
The survey responses give us relevant data including on life events from a sample of over 500 fine arts graduates; the interviews help us to locate and validate the range of personal meanings attached to transition and events (Heinz and Kruger, 2001).

We used an online survey for several reasons, among them speed of response and relative ease of collation.

The survey was initially emailed to 8,000 addresses via the alumni association. In total, we had a response rate of around 6.4 per cent, lower perhaps than we might have hoped. The length and complexity of the questionnaire may have dissuaded some, particularly its combination of open-ended 'write-in' questions and tick-box answers. However, including self-completion answers was a conscious trade-off, as is it allowed us to generate higher-quality data from the questionnaires.

Of the respondents willing to be interviewed, we eliminated overseas residents, for reasons of cost and practicality. From the rest, we constructed a sample which focused on key characteristics that we wished to investigate, based on the literature review.

The biographical interviews permit the innovation skills, attitudes and working practices of fine arts graduates to be examined in depth
By adopting a biographical approach for the interviews, we have been able to contextualise our graduates and examine other issues derived from the literature review, such as patterns of formal and informal learning and the attitudes that promote innovation, including resilience, risk-taking and a willingness to learn. By using 'turning points' and significant biographical events, we hope to get beneath simple description to see how both personal agency and institutional structures help to determine changes and outcomes.

Our methodology is based on grounded theory which allows interviewees themselves to describe what they see as innovations
Our approach to interviewing and analysis is based upon a notion of grounded theory (Charmaz, 2006). It enables respondents to identify what they see as 'turning points' relevant to them, rather than imposing an *a priori* notion of major changes (leaving school, university, first show and so on) as surveys alone would do. Similarly, 'innovations' (new media, new audiences, new work processes and so on) are described by the respondents

5. For a full description of the Research Methodology, please see Appendix 1.
6. For full survey results, please see Appendix 2.

in their own words and thus constructed by us from the data, not imposed upon it.

The interviews are semi-structured, relatively lengthy (one and a half to two hours) and conducted face-to-face. In them, we explore key themes for innovation (education, employment, markets and audiences), as well as those to do with 'personal life' (social networks, family life, attitudinal factors). As we are using biographical research methods (Gill, 2007), these issues are not separated in the interviews, but followed in a flexible, non-linear manner, so as to pursue each respondent's understanding. Using grounded theory also implies that each interview is slightly different from the last, building on insights gained from former interviews. The interviews thus construct a valuable body of material, rather than simply being 40 discrete, unrelated texts.

Part 4: Innovation in the arts world

4.1 Demography

The cohort on which this research is based is a group of over 500 members of the University of the Arts London (UAL) alumni association, who have graduated from the University's constituent colleges from the 1950s to the 2000s. Of these, 40 were selected for biographical interviews.

White females under the age of 50 and living in London are heavily represented in the survey sample

Almost three-quarters (72 per cent) of the sample is female and over half are under 50, with the majority being in their thirties and forties. The majority (79 per cent) live in the UK and are geographically concentrated – of these, 70 per cent live in greater London. Almost 80 per cent of those who responded described themselves as 'white'.

Consistent with other findings, average incomes are very low

Consistent with other surveys of the artistic workforce (Throsby and Hollister, 2003), incomes are relatively low. Less than 10 per cent of the sample earn over £50,000 per annum, while 30 per cent earn less than £10,000.

4.2 Sectors and occupations

Very large numbers are self-employed

As might be expected from a sample with large numbers of practising artists, some 70 per cent of survey respondents who work primarily in the cultural industries are self-employed, compared with only 7 per cent of those who work primarily in education. This compares with

an overall figure of 28 per cent self-employed in the creative industries (Higgs, Cunningham and Bakhshi, 2008).

Most are employed in the cultural and creative industries

Overall, just over 40 per cent of our questionnaire sample says that they work primarily in the arts and cultural industries; a further 6 per cent work in publishing and media, and around 11 per cent in design, crafts and new media. So, in total, almost 60 per cent of our graduates work in the wider cultural and creative sectors. A further 20 per cent work in education, 4 per cent in health care, with the remainder saying 'other'.

Again, this is consistent with the literature which suggests that those trained in the fine arts will endeavour to remain in them throughout their career (Throsby and Hollister, 2003; Aston, 1999; Blackwell and Harvey, 1999). But it also suggests that many of our graduates are indeed successful in remaining within them. The arts and cultural industries are of course a much bigger sector than the 'fine arts', but there seems to be a clear preference for work of a cultural nature.

Given the increased numbers of people studying fine arts and design – 60 per cent more over the past decade in the UK – one might expect that later generations would find it increasingly difficult to find employment in cultural occupations. However, an analysis of our survey respondents by decade of graduation suggests otherwise, at least for our sample (Table 1).

Art school graduates later in their working lives may either prefer to move into other sectors, or have to do so: the majority of younger

Table 1: Survey respondents by decade[7]

Decade of graduation	Percentage of sample working in arts and cultural industries
1960s	28.5 per cent
1970s	46.6 per cent
1980s	51.2 per cent
1990s	65.2 per cent
2000s	64.8 per cent

graduates, from the 1990s and 2000s, are still working in these areas. But it is also likely that the expansion of these sectors in the economy has meant that the growth in the number of jobs in these sectors has outpaced the number of graduates.

Given that sectoral categories are large, we also ask people to describe their occupations and in particular their current job titles, which gives us a clue to the nature of crossover. As respondents are asked to describe their current job title, rather than match it to a predetermined list, it is not uncommon for respondents to describe what they do rather than list a specific job title, making straightforward occupational categorisations difficult.

> "I have been leading a dual role lifestyle: artist and project director (voluntary basis), and information officer (publications)."
> (Female, 1980s graduate)

Indeed, almost 15 per cent of survey respondents write compound job titles, most of which include some type of artistic practice, for example "artist, facilitator, production assistant", and "painter/writer/illustrator".

Nearly 40 per cent of survey respondents hold second jobs
In our survey, consistent with other studies (Throsby and Hollister, 2003), nearly 40 per cent of people say that they currently hold second jobs. This percentage is broadly consistent across cohorts by decade of graduation.

Of those 40 per cent, around two in five hold a second job in the arts and cultural industries – suggesting that crossover is not just between the arts and other sectors, but as Throsby and Hollister (2003) suggest, "we observe a continuing blurring of occupational boundaries

within the arts, as artists acquire new skills and new interests, applicable across a range of artforms".

The interview evidence complicates this still further. What do we say of someone whose primary income comes from teaching in higher education, but whose 'artistic' work involves explorations of nanotechnology? Is this a teacher or an artist? Or does someone whose income is derived from arts-based therapy work in health care or the arts?

Categorising fine arts graduates by the sector of their employment can be difficult
This blurring of roles highlights the weaknesses of strong occupational categorisations within these sectors and points to a difficulty in quantifying the degree of crossover between the fine arts and other parts of the economy. At one extreme of the spectrum, there are survey respondents who work solely within fine arts practice. At the other, there are those who have given up artistic work to pursue other careers. But a majority – around 67 per cent – combine artistic and other work, for a variety of reasons.[8]

Very few fine arts graduates have only worked in fine arts throughout their careers
If we look over people's entire careers, which the interviews allow us to do, we see that even fewer people are likely only to have worked in fine arts or 'in the rest' of the economy. We could indeed argue that crossover happens continually throughout many artists' lives. This is discussed further in Section 4.8.

4.2.1 Being an artist or running a business?

Around 45 per cent of survey respondents have set up a business at some point in their working lives
Roughly 45 per cent of our survey respondents

7. This includes people working in the creative industry sectors as defined by the DCMS, but may also include a small number in engineering as the survey category is 'architecture and engineering'.

8. This seemingly sits oddly with the earlier finding that only around 40% of survey respondents claim to have second jobs. This means that some of those who claim to combine artistic work with other work do not view themselves as having more than one job.

Figure 1: Setting up a business by decade of graduation

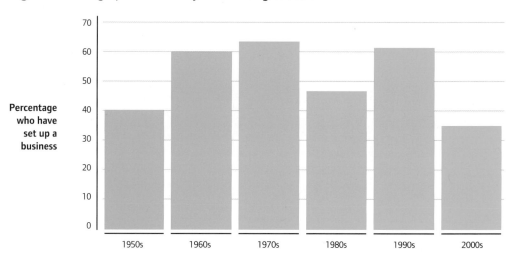

have set up a business at some point in their careers (with some fluctuation across cohorts by decade of graduation) – see Figure 1.

Those who have set up a business – surprisingly – provided similar answers to those who have not about working styles, promoting work and finding work: broadly the same percentage of both groups say their work is primarily self-initiated and they prefer to work independently.

Unsurprisingly, intellectual property issues are more important to those that have started their own businesses
However, some clues as to perhaps why they have set up a business come in their answers to a survey question about the relevance of Intellectual Property (IP) issues to them. Some 55 per cent of those who have set up a business say they have been relevant, compared with 33 per cent of those who have not.[9]

There is also some evidence of the role of public support in setting up businesses. This comes not from questions about business support however, but from the 58 per cent of those who have set up a business saying they have at some time been supported by benefits, a higher proportion than the 43 per cent of those who have not set up a business.

Interviewees single out income support and housing benefits as having supported them at key stages in their careers
More generally, our interviewees often reflect on the role that grants, benefits and subsidised

housing has played in their careers – a series of supports that many feel are no longer available to today's graduates.

*"I had a grant and then when I left school we could squat and get on the Enterprise Allowance Scheme and that was fantastic and everyone I knew there was an artist or a musician when I was doing that, actually. And that's what **we** did as well when we left Laban for a year, we got an Enterprise Allowance Scheme which gave us 40 quid a week each to live and we didn't have to sign on. People can't do that now."* (Female, 1970s graduate)

"Because of course in those days you didn't have to pay, I got full grants for my BA, and I got housing benefit, and I was living in a housing co-op, and I think I paid £6 a week or something, so it was doable basically. I was still in a housing co-op, but you also need to start paying for yourself and for your studio. Studios were a lot cheaper in those days as well." (Female, 1980s graduate)

4.3 Attitudes to innovation

Artists may seem like natural innovators
Artists may seem like natural innovators: they work in highly uncertain, inherently risky markets where originality is prized and 'imitation' often disparaged. But discussions of cultural production are rarely that simple. As Castañer and Campos (2002) point out, "in

9. Although equally we cannot rule out the possibility that those who identify IP issues as relevant do so because they have set up their businesses.

the arts world, there is no perfect substitution". In order to understand the role that fine arts graduates play in innovation, we analyse how they see innovation within their own work.

Survey respondents single out a "willingness to change or try new things" as their key attitudes

The survey does not probe attitudes to innovation specifically, as in-depth interviews are a better vehicle for collecting complex attitudinal issues. But we do ask people what factors are important in advancing their professional development (both within and outside the arts). Just over three quarters (76 per cent) of respondents mention, "willingness to change or try new things", an attitude clearly reflected in the quotes below.

Very few interviewees use the word 'innovation' itself

However, it is noticeable that very few of our interviewees ever use the term 'innovation', or related terms such as process or product innovation. This may be important for policy. If policymakers want to comprehend the role that the fine arts play within innovation, and develop policies that speak to the arts community, they may need to adopt appropriate language.

In analysing the interviews, we seek to draw out the differences between understanding of innovation, the processes of innovation and crossover.

But many fine arts graduates speak of the desire for novelty in their work

Although the term 'innovation' is very rarely used, respondents speak, on many occasions, about a desire for change or novelty in their own work, often allied to a dislike of repetition.

> "I don't like the idea of doing the same thing over and over again. I don't see the point once you've done something, or once someone has done something, in doing it again." (Female, 1970s graduate)

This is even the case where the work being 'repeated' has been creatively or economically successful:

> "I wouldn't do another Biba anyway. I just have no desire to replicate what you've done, there's no point, it's just so tiring doing things twice." (Male, 1960s graduate)

> "And I sold £10,000 worth of work which is quite a lot, but I was depressed, because

> to me I realised at that moment selling art wasn't my interest." (Male, 1980s graduate)

There is a temptation to characterise this as part of the 'artistic' identity (Bain, 2005); with people constantly seeking novelty and change. And respondents do often refer to their 'determination' or 'bloody mindedness'. But it would be mistaken to characterise this as an irrational process, or a search for novelty for its own sake. In fact, being willing to change is arguably a key part of the innovation mindset.

In some ways fine arts graduates demonstrate a high willingness to take risks in their careers

What is also being displayed is a willingness to take risky changes of direction, even when the status quo is economically successful. Indeed, some respondents speak of what one might see as a deliberate strategy or set of lifestyle choices that make such risk-taking possible; one describes her attitudes to personal finance "keeping overheads low". This enables her to cope with the insecurity of income that goes with self-employed artistic work.

For others, this may shade into self-exploitation where the need to earn a living is in constant battle with the need or desire to make art:

> "I didn't want to go full-time, because I'd actually, I'd made a promise to myself when I was on my degree, that I would never work full-time, because I could see that would be, that's the death knell to making art, because people start to get attached to their incomes, and it's much more difficult to take that step back." (Female, 1990s graduate)

Similarly, turning points are often described in terms of leaving what might be regarded as a safe option for a more risky one:

> "I ran the course there for four years, and it was great, was really healthy and I put a lot of work into it…and then I thought well you should go out on a real high so I resigned and moved to Hong Kong." (Female, 1990s graduate)

Or as one puts it simply:

> "I can handle the concept of permanent change in my working life." (Female, 1990s graduate)

4.3.1 Innovation and the market

Innovation research has long argued that spotting opportunities – or being open to change – are key characteristics of innovators. Rogers' observation (2003) that innovativeness is "the degree to which an individual is relatively earlier in adopting new ideas than other members of his social system," describes at least one part of the innovation process as reported by our respondents.

The artists studied show an acute awareness of the 'market' for their work

While Castañer and Campos (2002) argue that artists tend to take an essentially self-referential approach to definitions of innovation – seeing innovation as a change primarily in their own work – our artists' responses question this assertion. Although people often describe innovation in terms of their own work, this is often tied to an awareness of what else is in the 'market'.

Hence, as one performing artist says:

> "Actually recently we've been using also fragments of film that has a mood, a certain mood in it and we're trying to think why does this make us feel like that? What if we took something from this and something from that and put that together? What would happen? It's a kind of open-ended experiment…none of us can visualise the end product and we're not working towards something that's already established." (Female, 1970s graduate)

Here, the notion of what is 'already established' is essential to the nature of the experiment.

Artists' own consumption of culture is an important dimension of market awareness

As much of the literature argues (Becker, 1982; Bracewell, 2007; Lloyd, 2006), cultural workers are generally keen consumers of cultural products. This sometimes acts as a direct process of what we might call 'inspiration', as in the comments below:

> "I'm going back from two dimensional work into more three dimensional again and that's I think partly having seen the Louise Bourgeois exhibition." (Female, 1960s graduate)

> "I'd never read Dostoevsky till the last summer and it rained at Glastonbury and…so I spent ages in a tent and I read the whole of The Brothers Karamazov in like two days and I just got completely

obsessed…I've read them all now, and there's these moments in it that are very kind of odd and uncomfortable and I'm trying to work out why they're so strange and powerful, yet very upsetting. I'm collecting images that also cut into, resonate with that or have some tension with those ideas and then we talk together and make and come up with, well, let's do the complete works of Dostoevsky in, over ten nights." (Female, 1970s graduate)

But, more generally, it provides them with a context for the market in which they operate, and an awareness of it.

Even among the respondents who work solely within the fine arts, there are few totally autonomous, isolated individuals (Bain, 2005). As one practising sculptor commented, "it's really hard to make work without any assessment of it" (Female, 1970s graduate). We discuss the collaborative nature of artistic work and the degree to which feedback and critique matter in Section 4.5.

Awareness of the context or market in which one operates is rarely simple. Indeed the notion of the market itself is complex, and cannot always be equated with a place of commercial transactions. 'Audience' may be a better descriptor, as it can encompass fellow artists, critics, buyers, funders and direct end-users.

Nor should innovation be seen as a cultural product's only desirable quality (Bunting, 2007): tradition, heritage, memory and ritual influence the value that consumers get from cultural products, even in popular culture. Few fans at a Rolling Stones concert want to see the Stones take an entirely new musical direction; most come to hear old favourites and relive youthful memories. They are taking part in a communal ritual, not seeking novelty. However, at the same time, the production technology and skill required to reproduce a simulacrum of a recorded disc in a live setting – or the character of earlier performances – is considerable, and may be regarded as innovative.

For some artists the market acts as an 'ideal' user or something that can hone ideas

For some working within the fine arts, the 'market' becomes a sort of ideal user:

> "When I've got quite far into making something…I slightly worry about it because the ideal market or audience would

be young hip artists that think my work is really great, and big museum collectors. But quite often I make the work and think, oh that looks more like the audience might be small collectors, you know quite conservative. And then I think, oh God, how can I pull it back from that?" (Female, 2000s graduate)

In this case, perception of the market can be in tension with the production of work, a tension which the speaker attempts to resolve by imagining the reaction of her art school tutors:

"They'd probably go oh it's too flowery, it's too froo froo or something, so I think, right, I've got to make it less flowery then. So it's like they're the critic on my shoulder, I suppose, when I'm making work." (Female, 2000s graduate)

In this case the 'audience' of potential buyers or ex-tutors help to discipline and hone the artist's ideas.

Another artist describes how her contemporaries viewed her own turning point, when she moved from one form of artistic practice to another:

"So I left, and I thought people would just immediately forget, and they don't. And people were really cross that I'd left, and I had a collector, and I said, why is everybody so angry? He said, well, you were the marker…they don't know where they are any more, because you've disappeared, you were the marker of the boundary, and now you're not there, nobody knows where they are any more." (Female, 1970s graduate)

The market is also seen as a source of finance

In a few cases, the market is seen primarily in terms of funders. So changes in the type of work being funded, or the opening up of new areas of work such as regeneration and public art, can help produce a change of direction. The quotes below reflect conscious responses to funding priorities:

"Because obviously there's less and less money from the Arts Council. I mean I've always been successful with the Arts Council but I think it's time to get bigger money from someone else." (Female, 1990s graduate)

"What you find now is…avant-garde film makers are trying to get into the art world, because that's the only place where there's

funding recognition now." (Female, 1990s graduate)

4.3.2 Too innovative?

In some cases artists claim to be 'too innovative' for the market

In a few cases, innovation can be perceived as problematic for our respondents, particularly if it means their work cannot find a market or is 'too novel':

"I sort of think that I was one of the first people to do architectural installations really, and it was peculiar, because as opposed to now, where there's a massive context, there wasn't a context, you just struggled along… But there wasn't a market, and I think that if they'd been Young British Artists at that point, I would have been one of them, do you know what I mean?" (Male, 1960s graduate)

For others, the nature of that market problem may be more localised. One respondent working in design and marketing describes the effects of moving from a large city, where she regularly won public sector work, to a small town, where she felt the local authority was more conservative:

"We regularly get asked to pitch for work but we don't get it. I've been recently asking them why it is, why they keep asking us to tender, and we keep getting told that it's because we're too good, in terms of we're too innovative and people won't be, aren't ready for that sort of design." (Female, 2000s graduate)

4.3.3 Being innovative is not always perceived as being commercially successful

Artists' perceptions of what is and is not innovative does not always correspond to what is commercially successful

As we described in the literature review, the relationship between cultural production and innovation is complex; those who work in the fine arts may not perceive what they do to be innovation, regardless of how novel it is, or how much it produces a change in their own work.

One young fine artist described it thus:

"I think in itself it isn't innovation; it's just art work, which is slightly different. But I often think that if I moved it sideways I could, it could become an innovation of some sort." (Female graduate, 2000s)

In this case, innovation is being presented as what happens outside the arts, in other markets. Art work is seen as naturally changing. The danger with this approach again lies in artists' reluctance to describe their work as innovation; what happens inside the fine arts – change in product, markets or processes is presented as 'just art' – is hidden as innovation.

As we have seen, respondents often consciously decided not to do something, even if it would be commercially successful:

"Because I was never really good at doing two things that were the same…so I knew that I wasn't a painter in terms of, I couldn't really make a living out of having to choose a style and then work to it." (Female, 2000s graduate)

In this case, being successful is seen to mean repetition, constraining innovation. Adopting an apparently uncommercial attitude can also enable people to take chances, as one young man about to open a gallery commented:

"I'm fortunate that I don't have to pander too much, and we're not, we're never going to be a big West End gallery, we're not even going to be an East End gallery, just like a tiny little hole in South East London, but I think that can be, I think that in its own right could be quite interesting. And particularly because I have the freedom to be able to choose completely what I, what I would like to do with it. It's quite a gamble, I have no idea how successful it's going to be, but it's an interesting one." (Male, 2000s graduate)

4.4 Skills for innovation

Previous research asserts links between art education and wider critical thinking

As discussed in the literature review, recent work on innovation (Lester and Piore, 2004) argues that artists are particularly important in 'third generation innovation' due to their particular training, their disposal towards critical thinking and their close understanding of consumer needs.

Lampert (2006) argues that there may well be a link between art education and critical thinking because art students practise reflective thinking and aesthetic inquiry, both when they create artwork and when they discuss their own and others' work. Few empirical studies have tested this link, although Lampert refers to one, by Burton, Horowitz and Abeles (2000), which finds that students with high arts exposure show a greater understanding of "multiple or alternative vantage points".

This is borne out by the perceptions of the fine arts graduates in our study

As one interviewee, now working as a consultant in the software industry says, when discussing the 'crit' process:

"And that was the key piece of rigour that we got, standing up for yourself… From a consultant point of view, you want to be sure that you don't suggest…here's something broken and here's my proposed solution. You actually have to take that person to believe your proposed solution is right for them…every person at (that) art school has the articulacy and the commitment to be able to talk in that way. And I think it actually stands a lot of us in very good stead going forwards, if we don't even realise that's the thing that we're being taught." (Male, 2000s graduate)

While another, who also works in the software industry, adds:

"You have to be so driven and focussed as an artist. You've decided to do whatever it is you've decided to do. Sculpture or whatever. So if it doesn't work, you've got two choices. You can abandon it, but if you're going to abandon it that quickly, why did you decide to do it in the first place? Or you can find a solution to the problem. So you're more motivated to do that." (Female, 1990s graduate)

Art education is also seen to foster communication skills and teamwork

Willingness to put one's work on show, to accept constructive criticism and to let that feed the development of future ideas, are obviously part of this process. But critical to its success is the community of practice (Wenger, 1998) where it takes place. Communication skills, teamwork and emotional intelligence, which some argue are developed in arts

Table 2: Top skills learned from fine arts education

| What skills have you learned from your fine arts education? (Top 3 answers) | | | | | |
1950s	1960s	1970s	1980s	1990s	2000s
1. Aesthetic appreciation (60%)	1. Aesthetic appreciation (90%)	1. Analytical and critical reasoning (91%)	1. Aesthetic appreciation (94%)	1. Analytical and critical skills (90%)	1. Analytical and critical reasoning (83%)
1. To work independently (60%)	1. To work independently (90%)	2. Aesthetic appreciation (89%)	2. To work independently (91%)	2. To work independently (88%)	1. Theoretical skills (83%)
2. Analytical and critical skills (40%)	2. To create original works (80%)	2. To work independently (89%)	3. To create original works (89%)	3. Aesthetic appreciation (77%)	2. To work independently (81%)
2. Theoretical skills (40%)	3. Technical skills (75%)	3. To create original works (86%)			3. Aesthetic appreciation (75%)
2. Technical skills (40%)					

Note: the percentages refer to the proportion of respondents who ticked the skills stated

programmes (Bryce *et al.*, 2004), are invaluable in forming and sustaining such communities. Lampert's findings may also explain why the process of socialisation (who you know, rather than what you know) is more important in many creative and cultural industries than formal education (Bathelt *et al.*, 2004).

In the survey, we ask people an open-ended question about skills and attributes, particularly those learned at art school. Respondents are allowed to choose as many from the list as they want and also to write in answers. The answers show a remarkable consistency across generations (Table 2).

We do not ask people to rank these skills in this question. But responses to other questions in the survey do not suggest that those who rate particular skills highly behave systematically any differently from others. For example, 41 per cent of those who say that 'working independently' is the most important skill they have learned at art school are self-employed; almost the same as the whole cohort. And these individuals appear to be no more likely to seek out informal training or undertake self-initiated work. In addition, of those whose primary job is outside the cultural sectors – in health care or education – a similar percentage of people say that they work independently.

It is striking that very few survey respondents mention technical skills as being the most important thing they have learned
A striking aspect of the survey responses, however, is that very few respondents cite technical skills as the most important thing they have learned (though aesthetic appreciation ranks very highly and while far from a 'technical' skill it may be considered the most culturally-specific skill mentioned).

Large numbers claim to have participated in informal and formal training during their careers
What may matter more from an innovation perspective is the degree to which people's education enables them to develop the skills of lifelong learners (Seltzer and Bentley, 1999). Overall, almost 44 per cent of survey respondents say they have received formal training of some kind after fine arts study and just under 80 per cent of respondents overall say that they have participated in informal learning since completing their fine arts studies.

One might expect that the sector in which people work affects access to training, but this does not appear to be the case with our sample. For example, of those with a primary occupation in the arts/cultural industries, 40 per cent of people report undertaking formal training after graduating; but roughly the same proportion of those who work outside these sectors in their primary jobs have participated in formal training too. (However, as expected, those whose primary job is in education are more likely to have received funding for formal training, 73 per cent of them report having some).

Participation in informal learning is particularly high for those in the arts and cultural industries

Participation in informal learning is high across all sectors of primary employment – in the arts and cultural industries and education, in particular. Only in the health care/medical sector does the percentage who have taken part in informal learning after graduation drop to 50 per cent – this probably reflects the sector's more formal knowledge base and training opportunities.

Respondents with a second job are much more likely to have participated in formal training

Second-job holding seems to be associated with greater propensity to undertake formal training. Respondents with a second job are much more likely to have participated in formal training: over half (55 per cent) versus 38 per cent of those without a second job.

4.4.1 Art school – learning by asking around?

Both our survey and interview evidence suggest that the experience of art school is highly influential in developing lifelong learning skills, and is often seen as critical to the development of fine arts graduates' skills and work practices. Research on the cultural industries often downplays the experience of formal education (Timms and Wright, 2007) – even Sectors Skills Councils appear sceptical[10] – but those in the fine arts tell a somewhat different story.

As Frith and Horne note in their study of the links between art schools and popular music (Frith and Horne, 1987):

> "The art school is unique in British higher education. It condones and encourages an attitude of learning through trial and error, through day-to-day experiment, rather than through instruction."

The fine arts graduates stress the importance of relatively unstructured learning and peer review in their art education

Although there have been significant changes in art school education in the 20 years since

this was written, particularly with the greater number of students in higher education, this distinctive stress on relatively unstructured learning, aided but not directed by peers, assistants and tutors, remains a striking feature of our graduates' experiences.

Many describe their time at art school as an act of self-creation, where art was not so much taught, as learned through personal discovery. Older graduates describe this:

> "But, in fact, at that time I can remember when we first started oil painting, the teacher gathered us into the room and he said, now, he said, you all know how to paint in oils, he said, just get going and that was it." (Female, 1950s graduate)

> "So art school training doesn't necessarily make you a better painter, because it's difficult to teach actually the technique of painting. It's for you to discover and you to find out, so again that actual act and enquiry, I think, is a very good thing in the future, that you're not given things on a plate. You have to go and get them and you have to find out, you have to have an enquiring mind, you have to know where to go and get information about subjects." (Male, 1960s graduate)

And so do more recent graduates:

> "But at St Martins you were left to fend for yourself a lot, but you were also watched over in a way as well. So it was sort of about experimentation I think. And I think it's a really good way to learn actually, because if you get left with a load of paint and a bit of wood and stuff, and you don't really know what to do with it, you're going to make your own world out of it, aren't you, if you've got any imagination?" (Female, 2000s graduate)

So, arts students learn by asking around

In turn, this produces a high degree of what one might call 'learning by asking around', an approach made possible by the sociability of working all day with other students in a studio (as opposed to a library or lecture room):

> "The act of, the constant artistic environment that you're in, because don't forget you are in it every day, you should be anyway, with tutors who are experts at their job. It's not like university where you go to the library and then you have a tutorial once a week. This is every day. You're

10. See http://www.ccskills.org.uk/news/story.asp?pageid=964&siteID=1&pageTypeID=

surrounded sociably, you're in it." (Male, 1960s graduate)

One interviewee who has studied both social sciences and fine arts at university (and now teaches social science) notes the difference in this way of learning and her current way of working in higher education:

"Well I think maybe it goes back to the space thing, I don't know whether it's kind of spatial because that feeling was definitely associated with being in a workshop and when I'm up in my room (now), and my work is just reams of paper, or it's on the computer, you can't, it's just not, there's not that minute by minute sharing that you can do in a studio." (Female, 2000s graduate)

Tutors and technicians play different roles
Another factor which may influence this style of learning is the differing role of tutors and technicians in art school and the way they interact with students. Many students reflect on the extent to which developing skills, particularly technical skills, results from interaction, particularly with technicians:

"They came in with the Coldstream Report I think, differentiation between technicians and teachers and basically what it meant was that the teachers, most of them, gave up teaching technique, but freelancers often talked technique... The technicians were there for the technique. So in fact most of my skills were picked up, I picked up from the technicians and they were terrific." (Male, 1960s graduate)

"You could sign up with technicians for an hour here and there doing this and that, and they were the ones that I learnt a few technical skills from. But mostly you're left to your own devices, and you have to be sort of self sufficient and independent. I remember one of the technicians, I'd go up and say I've got this really good idea I want to make, I want to make like a volcano in the studio, and he'd go OK, well everyone can have an idea, but how are you going to do it?" (Female, 2000s graduate)

The quote above nicely illustrates the specific nature of this educational formation. Technical skills are acquired as and when needed to complete a particular task; the speaker describes attitudinal factors – 'self sufficiency and independence' – as necessary, but the

encounter is still primarily about 'making' the practical realisation of an idea.

4.4.2 The role of technical skills

Technical skills are important, but less so than conceptual skills
The stress or otherwise on specific technical skills, as opposed to cognitive skills, at art school remains a contested area among our respondents. Technical skills were mentioned by around 75 per cent of graduates in every decade from the 1960s until the 2000s, making them important, but less so than more conceptual skills.

However, the interviews suggest greater complexity. For example, there is some variation in responses across cohorts: older graduates seem largely unconcerned by the lack of formal focus on technical skills when they were at college, probably partly because technicians were around to help them develop these skills, when they were needed for producing work.

Some more recent graduates, however, resent what they see as a lack of focus on technical skills training at undergraduate level:

"I would love to be able to screen print, I'd love to be able to just do basic form of a screen, photographic screen prints, and it's such a simple technique. I know it's an interesting technique, but it's one that I can't possibly master on my own just through trial and error, it's not even physically possible to have that kind of set up, and you need a print studio." (Male, 2000s graduate)

There may be many reasons why more recent graduates have a stronger focus on specific technical skills. They are less likely to be established in their careers and memories of educational experiences are fresher. It is also possible to detect a more 'consumerist' attitude among recent graduates – many of whom have had to go into debt to fund their higher education.

Technical skills matter most to those working within the fine arts
However, the interviews show that specific technical skills, perhaps unsurprisingly, are valued by those working within the fine arts.

"Art is determined by your skill base actually, as a practitioner you tend to rely

a lot on a range of skill base that you can access. Either because you're confident in a wide range of skills or because you know somebody you can learn off, and the narrower that is, that's going to affect your work." (Female, 1980s graduate)

4.4.3 Boundary spanners

The attitudes acquired in art education stand those who have crossed over in good stead

For those who have 'crossed over', either into other cultural industries or elsewhere, it is the 'thinking skills' or attitudes that they learned which appear to matter most. The value of 'boundary spanners' is well recognised in the innovation literature (Dodgson, Gann and Salter, 2005); these are people who can search across organisational and disciplinary boundaries for solutions and are expert at transmitting knowledge to where it is needed. We find many elements of this cross-disciplinary or boundary spanning in our respondent accounts.

One 1960s graduate, who ending up working in design, comments:

"I do think that, I think I was very lucky to have the freedom to go through an entirely professional career not actually being trained in anything."

As he explains about his approach to design:

"I think, we've always been known, not because we had a different style but because we had a different attitude. Because we are not trained we don't have a preconception as to what design is. So if someone says to us, I want a food hall, I'm rushing off doing baked bean tins that are 7ft 6 tall, and cross sections of archaeological digs that are the wine cellar and things and other people are thinking about racking. Yeah? See, I don't give a bugger about racking, I'm making people laugh. I'm designing the 12th century cattle and dairy area of a Normandy farm that's got a freezer in it that when you pick up a yoghurt, the cows go moo, which I think's great, that's design." (Male, 1960s graduate).

While another fine artist, who moved into performance arts, comments:

"I could take the rules of art school in how to develop yourself and your thoughts and your art work and just shift that over to movement. And actually I think that's why from that point I've always been very interested in taking the model of X and applying it to Y." (Female graduate, 1980s)

In other cases, the boundary-spanning is more dramatic, for example from fine arts into psychotherapy:

"I just knew there was something about the illusion of what's on a two dimensional surface, the dialectical tension between 2D and 3D or the illusion of 3D. And the whole business of what's revealed and what's hidden so there were germs of what I was struggling with at the time... And it's only with analysis and knowing what I do know that I can look into them and find what's there probably and I can revisit some of what I was trying to do then but with more awareness. I can work it now so it kind of pulls together, as you say, there is quite an overlap between therapy and the artwork, yeah, most definitely." (Female, 1960s graduate)

Or into sciences:

"I'd identified within my own work, there were a number of scientific concerns... so I read around lots of things to do with memory and various bits and pieces, and then I want to see who was researching some of these areas in the country. And there were a couple of people I identified, and one chap who was doing things to do with visual perception...I was really interested in the things that he'd written and so I just sent him an email and said look I've sent you some images here as an attachment, I'm really interested in what you do, this is what I do, these are some of the interests that I have, what do you reckon? And he was great and he came back and said fantastic let's catch up. And it was just a collaboration that was just perfect from day one." (Female, 1990s graduate)

The social process involved – identifying an interest or need; identifying the person or persons who can be helpful; and then contacting them – is familiar from most of the other accounts.

4.5 Networks and innovation processes

Innovation is not usually for loners
While respondents often describe their attitudes to innovation in terms of an individual response, the process of innovation itself is almost always social. Even the most self-contained painter or sculptor needs other human 'resources' (Becker, 1982).

In this section, we look at how innovations happen, both through the survey responses and in the words of our interviewees.

4.5.1 Attitudes to networking

Interviewees had mixed views about networking
As both the survey evidence and interviews show, attitudes to both the need to network and its effectiveness are complex. Networking is seen as necessary, but people may personally find it uncomfortable. But some see it as the only way to get on.

Survey questions about the importance of networking, not surprisingly, produce overwhelmingly positive answers. Almost 90 per cent who work in the arts and cultural sectors consider networking within the arts important.

Almost three quarters, 73 per cent, of those working in the arts/cultural industries consider networking outside these industries as important too. Survey respondents had no opportunity to explain their answers, but interview evidence suggests that it arises from the combination of a cross-fertilisation of skills and ideas, the possibility of new markets and enriching one's art work with external influences.

Networks rank low among career advancement factors, but provide important sources of encouragement
However, when the survey asks what has been important in advancing people's careers, the top four answers are: experience (74 per cent); opportunities to exhibit work (74 per cent); university/art college education (73 per cent) and natural talent (73 per cent); nobody mentions networks.

Yet, when listing sources of encouragement for arts work, 'peers' are quoted most often – again emphasising the importance of collaborative networking and the role of the network as support, rather than just what has been important in advancing one's career.

The different emphases in these answers show the complexities that networking provokes in the minds of fine artists. A write-in survey answer reflects this ambivalence: "I think it is important, but it is something I hate to do, as it makes me feel insincere", said one female graduate. Others in the survey seem to regard it somewhat more cynically: "In fact success is reliant upon knowing the correct people and not upon talent", another observed.

Networking is also good for business, but may not work for everyone
This ambivalence is again picked up by interviewees:

> "Well just, either through networking, actually not really through networking, because we hate networking, but through people we know really, family, friends and things like that. But then it became, people who we met at…through…just through stuff." (Female, 2000s graduate)

Here there is clearly a reluctance to use the term networking. Yet "family, friends and things like that" are essential to making this small design business work. The quote is also revealing of the wider debate about diversity in these sectors – the notion that one's family, friends and "things like that" can get you access to work and help your career is unlikely to apply across the social spectrum.

4.5.2 Collaboration and networking

Networking organisations are seen as providing social support rather than influence
Another way to look at networks is through the membership of professional associations. Some 64 per cent of respondents belong to an artist organisation, studio or collective. However, when we ask them how this influences their work, answers focus less on the influence of such organisations and more on the social support they offer, "a good chance to meet and talk to like-minded people".

When interviewees describe processes of collaboration, networking is also described, not just in terms of career advancement, but also again in terms of support (Currid, 2007), reinforcing the importance of feedback and critique.

"I often end up working with some of my colleagues who I did the course with and we help each other out and we give each other work if we can't do a job, whatever." (Female, 1990s graduate)

"I just know people who run small cabarets and things still, social circle, and we talk about the kinds of work that I want to do. I've got a little network of people, who know what I do and are trying to find a way of it benefiting them and their customers, their regulars and me." (Female, 1970s graduate)

The ethos of an artistic identity appears important here:

"I give that information very freely to other people and in return I do expect other people to give me information. We're very sharing, artists, I think." (Female, 2000s graduate)

Leaving London requires the establishment of new networks

As we see below in the section on geography, respondents pursuing an artistic career who move outside London face the challenge of re-establishing a network of practitioners, not just for instrumental needs, but for feedback and support. One recent graduate describes the process of moving out of college/London and having to set up new networks:

"Well, it, and it's funny because with the MA, obviously there's that peer group...and obviously a few of us are still in touch, in terms of exhibitions going on and private viewings and I did, you'd try to keep a certain momentum and then it fades a little bit. But also it's quite a nice way to actually, creating your own network...from either setting up projects yourself, or to contribute in ways in which your voice can be heard. But I think, yeah, it's good to have that, certainly of, support, or feel that you're connected with other artists." (Female, 2000s graduate)

Another, who had previously trained overseas and moved to London, describes why she went to art school:

"What was lacking when I came here in my life was interaction you know. So I thought this would be the best way to get a feedback and just talk about my work." (Female, 2000s graduate)

4.5.3 Networking and 'chance' meetings

Networking is particularly important for organising work practices
While the term 'networking' provokes ambivalent reactions, the importance of networks in the cultural industries is a result of the organisation of working practices; the particularity of project-based working, with high levels of self employment and freelancing, requires constant 'keeping in touch' both in work and outside it.

Both formal networks (such as professional groupings or artists' associations) and informal networks (friends and colleagues) play a large role. Around three-quarters of respondents who work primarily in the arts and cultural industries are members of professional organisations compared with around half who work outside.

Contacts, chance meetings and recommendations are of great value
But what does this notion of networking actually mean in practice? In the interviews, processes of change are often described in social terms, generally as a result of contacts with friends, chance meetings and recommendations.

"And then a friend of mine phoned me up and said, I'm doing all these murals in Germany, do you want to come along?" (Female, 1990s graduate)

This quote is essentially reproduced many times. One refers to this as 'ground networking':

"It's through that kind of ground networking of people...you just find out what your friends do and you go, that sounds a good job. If one comes up give it to me." (Female, 1980s graduate)

Chance meetings are often described as turning points by respondents, as the following quotes demonstrate.

"I met Barbara and Fitz and they were talking to me over dinner one night and I was going on, and I said that I was doing various bits of design, and I was getting out of the music industry and going to set up my own studio. And Barbara just said, we've got, we're doing this new store on Kensington High Street and we need someone to do the children's department,

but not just design it but also build it. And, I said, I can do that." (Male, 1960s graduate)

"Then one of the exhibitions that we had, a friend who's an artist who also had another friend and was at the Wellcome Trust and they just happened to come along to the exhibition and this man then came up to us afterwards and said, I run the...at Wellcome Trust and I really like what you do, would you put a proposal in to the Wellcome Trust?" (Female, 1980s graduate)

"And then about two years ago (my family come from Cumbria), I decided to do a local artist in residence, sort of open studios in Cumbria because I hadn't done anything in Cumbria for ages… So I went, did this artists in residence, open studio thing, and I just was in a space near where the exhibition was…surprisingly, someone came in and said, would you like to be artist in residence at Kathmandu University?" (Female, 1980s graduate)

But chance meetings are not entirely random

These and similar incidents reveal that 'chance meetings' are not completely random. Social networks, geography and timing play a role, as do attributes like self confidence ('I can do that'). A core element, as described above, is being able to 'open up and talk to people'.

One respondent who works in the music industry says:

"I found that any kind of breaks I did get was through, not being pushy but putting yourself about, and being out and about, and doing things and meeting people, not waiting to be discovered. But then, that's music isn't it?" (Male, 1970s graduate)

It would appear that not only is it music, but even within the fine arts, similar processes are at work.

4.5.4 The role of 'significant others'

Teachers, friends and family are often a source of encouragement

An important variant on chance meetings is interaction with particularly significant others – people in one's life who can help facilitate turning points. For many of our respondents, such people – parents, teachers or friends of the family – are significant in the decision to study art.

In our survey, parents/caregivers, school teachers and peers are given as the primary source of encouragement for studying art in each decade.

One interviewee says:

"She said, you've got an eye for perspective and I think it was probably one of those moments. I enjoyed doing art but nobody had really said, that sounds really awful doesn't it? Nobody said I was good at anything before then. But that somebody, somebody that wasn't my mum and dad, who was a practising artist had said to me, you can do that." (Female, 1990s graduate)

In other cases, a significant other is the person who spots a different opportunity within existing work:

"I go to every show and I photograph every show with the idea that it will be interesting to take pictures of the movement that's made from still images, and then re-use it to make more movement, so take pictures of the moments between the pictures. But that was for my own use and then somebody saw them and said this would make an interesting thing and I realised it is actually quite a bizarre view and a unique view, so I've agreed to do that." (Female, 1970s graduate)

Or a relationship which leads to a change of direction:

"I helped to run the Film Society at Cardiff, and I, so we watched lots of films. And then I got involved in some of my art work where the installation pieces looked like film sets, and actually were to do with relating architecture to movie images, and so on. And then in the 80s, when I was teaching at Chelsea, it was just at the birth of the pop video, and one of my students had become involved with that world." (Male, 1970s graduate)

Again, what is being described here is a mix of social networks, skills and work experience, and timing.

4.5.5 Reputation effects

The success of chance encounters can depend on one's reputation

One factor that enables seemingly chance encounters to 'work' is the role of reputation.

Networks within cultural industries (and beyond them) are essentially reputational communities (Pratt, 2006), where formal processes play a relatively weak role. For those within these sectors this can prove problematic. As one respondent who works in theatre says:

> "But generally I don't get jobs when I apply in that way (answering an advertisement), or I might get an interview, but normally jobs are word of mouth, where you don't even have to show your work to somebody, they accept the word of the person who's recommended you. It's very hard to control, it's quite frustrating." (Female, 1980s graduate)

And another observes:

> "And you can't ever phone up a curator cold, if you do you have to do it because someone's recommended you, and you also know three other people that they know who think you're great too, and they may have spoken about you, so you phone up on that basis." (Female, 1990s graduate)

And this may require alternative networking arrangements
This highlights a dilemma faced by policymakers in the cultural industries. To what extent should policy go with the grain of the sectors and support social networks and the development of reputation? And to what extent should it try to counteract what can be both a socially exclusive process and a potential barrier to progression?

Concerns about lack of diversity in the cultural labour force (Knell and Oakley, 2007) have led to DCMS proposals for apprenticeship schemes and other interventions to provide more formal – and potentially more open – pathways into employment in this field (DCMS, 2008).

While the debate is sometimes posed as being about public policy interfering with the 'ways things are done' in the cultural sectors (Timms and Wright, 2007), these remarks suggest that not everyone within the cultural industries is happy with the way things are done.

4.6 Creativity and innovation – is everything culture?

In Section 2, we introduced the 'culturisation' thesis, which argues for the increasing role of culture in the production of non-cultural objects. In this section, we consider what our study can tell us about this thesis.

First, we consider the degree to which the expansion of cultural markets has affected the working lives of our respondents; and second, we consider whether this means that we can collapse the distinctions between cultural and non-cultural activities.

4.6.1 The growth of cultural markets

More and more graduates work in the arts and cultural industries
As Table 1 showed, an increasing proportion of graduates say they work in the arts and cultural industries. Many accounts suggest that this is likely to reflect the growth of these sectors over the last fifty years (Andari et al., 2007); that period has also seen a broadening of what might be considered cultural activities – from the growth of whole new cultural forms like videogames, to the diversification of existing activities and creation of new sub-categories like public or installation art.

There are important links to popular music
The art school has often been portrayed as the core educational foundation (Bracewell, 2007; Frith and Horne, 1987) for much of British popular culture and music. A roll call of 1960s pop musicians who graduated from London art colleges alone would include: Keith Richard, Ron Wood, Peter Townsend, Freddie Mercury, Eric Clapton, Syd Barrett, Jeff Beck, Ray Davies, Jimmy Page and Charlie Watts. This list ignores non-London luminaries like John Lennon. A similar list for the punk era would include Paul Simenon and Mick Jones of the Clash, Ian Dury, Siouxsie Sioux, Billy Idol, Pete Shelley and Howard Devoto.

It is thus unsurprising that many of our interviewees have worked in the expanding cultural industries – from reggae music to TV.

> "I'd also been involved in bands, performing, making movement sequences and sometimes singing or playing some kind of percussion with various groups of musicians which also fed into what I was doing." (Female, 1970s graduate)

One graduate who moved into dance, but acknowledges that her business model reflected her observation of pop musicians, remembers:

"In a band the ethos was that it was quite expected that everyone would go along… They'd have some kind of work and pay their share of rehearsal costs and transportation costs for gigs. So I took that mentality and thought that's all I knew… So we each had to pay 20 quid each a week into the company and that would pay for costumes and costs and we'd go in guerrilla style, running the, use a place or churches would let us rehearse sometimes." (Female, 1970s graduate)

Links exist with other cultural forms too

For others, a hobby or enthusiasm for another cultural form is linked to their own work.

"Nick Adams who was in my year at art school and I were taking photos and I heard there was a stall selling records up the road. So I went up there after I'd done the photos…and then got chatting to the people… It was reggae, so that was all we did, that's all we were interested in. Used to import records, sell them on the stall at first…but we ended up with two shops, a distribution, a record label, a studio. Everything really, really took off in the 80s and the 90s." (Male, 1970s graduate)

Another graduate explains how she and her partner use their gallery cum home to play music:

"When we moved in here, we did have, we went off on a bit of a side track and we were putting on techno gigs in the basement for a couple of friends that are really, really good techno DJs and this gave us a way of supporting them." (Female, 1980s graduate)

Public policy-led markets have played an important role

Public policy-led markets for the arts have been important for employment of fine artists, particularly in urban regeneration, public art and health care.

One graduate talks about how, in a way that he describes as "completely crazy", he became an employee in the health care sector:

"My wife by this time had gone back to work and was working for Islington Health Authority and a post came up there, which is completely crazy and I can't imagine how it ever came about, but it was when the local authority and the health authorities were linking more…and they set up a unit

as part of their health education work which was a media unit which was shooting films, slide, tape presentations, posters, booklets, exhibitions, and I got the job running this little unit." (Male, 1960s graduate)

Another talked of the work she and her partner had done with the London Borough of Hackney:

"It was a big paid job but it's still within our art… We had a big regeneration job with Hackney Council… We learned loads of stuff. How to deal with councils, how contractors work." (Female, 1980s graduate)

It is interesting that, when describing their work with Hackney, this graduate also uses the phrase "it's still within our art", meaning that the work itself is cultural, even if the end product in this case is not. Similarly, while the end product in the former case is better health information, this respondent's work is producing films, posters and books. This draws attention to the differences between what might be considered cultural and non-cultural work and poses interesting questions for the culturisation thesis.

4.6.2 Culture and creativity

'Creativity' rather than 'innovation' is the preferred term among fine artists

As might be expected from those trained in the fine arts, respondents are more likely to use the term 'creativity' than they are to use 'innovation'. Thus their language differs from that favoured by policymakers. They rarely use the term 'creative industries', with respondents preferring to talk either about the arts or their own particular field, such as sculpture or photography.

Creativity, when it is used, generally describes a process, not a product. Respondents are thus more likely to talk about 'being creative' in their approach to work, rather than about producing a 'creative' output.

One respondent now working in health care, describes her experience of art school:

"I certainly learned how to think much more creatively, much more laterally, about things and objects, and sometimes to redefine the nature of the object. So a pair of pliers can be an implement to cut through materials with, but tie it to a piece of string and

hang it from somewhere, and it becomes a weight." (Female, 1960s graduate)

Here the object is a pair of pliers; only the approach to it is creative. Another respondent distinguishes between creativity and the arts:

"I am a creative. But that's just how I think. But I'm not an artist, I don't make work, I don't sell work, I don't exhibit. I think like an artist, I'm an artist at home, I'm an artist in my head, but not on paper." (Female, 2000s graduate)

Process matters more than products for creativity

This stress on process rather than products exposes one difficulty with the notion of the creative industries. Creativity in these interviews does not reside in an object (still less an industry). And those who have moved outside of the fine arts are no less likely to talk about creativity than those within them. One respondent, who works for a software company, says:

"It was creative problem solving and I guess, I brought a creative approach to the business. Which in some ways I find more creative than sitting and doing a drawing. It uses more parts of my brain I'd almost say." (Female graduate, 2000s)

Another says:

"Then I moved over to the (gallery x), into a more focused database manager role, and I learnt a lot there about how, it's funny, it has a reputation of being a much, much more creative institution but was much, much less creative to work in at various levels where you've, I was quite constrained. So I was quite creative at (gallery y) in how I changed the things that were in my immediate work environment, whereas at the (gallery x) you were told, yeah, you can be creative, but only if the director agrees with you." (Male graduate, 2000s)

In this case, the speaker is working in a 'non-creative' occupation, but within a cultural institution – a characterisation which itself shows how difficult occupational and other classifications can be in this area (Higgs, Cunningham and Bakhshi, 2008).

Creativity, for our speakers, is not synonymous with culture or the arts. Artistic work can either be creative or formulaic; non-artistic work can similarly be creative or otherwise. There is no perception that work in other parts of the economy is necessarily less creative. But at the same time, the distinctions between cultural work and non-cultural work tend to be retained by these speakers.

One respondent, talking about his work as an artist, says:

"It's vocational work…absolutely, it almost serves no purpose in a sense…you don't have a very literal purpose, like if you were training to be a lawyer, or a solicitor, or a doctor." (Male, 2000s graduate)

Here, the notion of culture as something created for its own sake is being contrasted with other types of work. Such 'purposelessness' can be used to distinguish art from design, though not necessarily to privilege it:

"We think of art as being this thing that, it's like soul food and it nourishes you in some kind of deep way but actually there may be a chair that is beautiful to look at and incredibly comfortable to sit on and brings a smile to your face whenever you see or conjures up some memory from childhood. It can do all the things that art can do and it performs a function." (Female, 2000s graduate)

In this case, the speaker again stresses the distinctiveness of art, even though a beautiful chair may offer many of the same benefits. For these speakers there are limits to 'culturisation'; a running shoe may have cultural inputs and be worked on by culturally-trained workers. But it is not a piece of art.

4.7 Geography and the London effect

London as the cultural capital – the impact of distance and class

In the survey, more than 70 per cent of respondents who reside in the UK live in Greater London. Our study provides some support for the arguments advanced in the literature on cultural industries and place.

For example, the interviews provide testimony to the role of symbolic capital – in this case the symbolic capital of London – not only in terms of people's work practice but even more as a location for art schools.

One graduate sums it up as follows:

"St Martins, London, Soho; that's art in my head." (Male, 1980s graduate)

For many graduates, this presented a significant journey, both in distance...:

"Most definitely, if you were going to go on to art school, you went to London. And my art teacher suggested I apply to Camberwell School, which I did, and I came to London for an interview. I'd never been to London before and so going to Camberwell for this interview was quite a big event for me." (Male, 1960s graduate)

"I grew up in Devon and I desperately wanted to come to London where everything was and you've obviously got all the galleries and the life and the culture and, you know... It seemed like the appropriate place to study art where a lot of artists were." (Female, 2000s graduate)

...and in terms of social class:

"I was born in Southall just outside London, working class background... Now, though I was in a suburb, in those days coming from a suburb was quite a thing. You did it Christmas and things like that, it wasn't a thing you did all the time. My parents never had a car in their life, and it was an overland train, there was no underground." (Male, 1960s graduate)

The impact of the swinging sixties on artists
The extent to which these expectations were fulfilled reflects personal experience. But there are, as might be expected, particular eras when London seemed to be at the centre, not just of the fine arts world, but of a wider cultural world. The 1960s is an obvious, heavily mythologized, example of this:

"So there I was aged 17 on the King's Road, Chelsea, saying Yes!" (Male, 1960s graduate)

"And I think I was lucky with the timing, that's when the Beatles were well on the rise, the exhibition where I worked for Yoko was the one she met John Lennon, down at Indica Gallery and they came to the college and did their black bag piece, which she was in the middle of doing things like this at that time." (Female, 1960s graduate)

For others, the same experience is recalled somewhat differently:

"It was, the 60s was the period of sexual liberation so there was an awful lot of happenings, stuff which was really just silly...it was a period when to shock seemed to be a thing to do but I never wanted to do that. So I think I felt somewhere in the back of my mind I probably wouldn't make a massive splash as an artist in that sort of way." (Male, 1960s graduate)

New media and movements in the eighties and nineties
The growth of popular cultural forms – pop music, video, TV and latterly, new media – all provided openings for art school graduates, including some of our respondents.

The late 1980s and early 1990s, with the rise of the 'Young British Artists' (YBAs) presented a similar 'moment' in some respects, though one that was perhaps more directly concerned with the growth of a commercial market for fine arts in particular.

One of our respondents, a student in the early 1990s says:

"Yeah, in London at that time you could kind of do anything." (Female, 1990s graduate)

Changing culture leads to new markets
These moments matter not only because people experienced them, but because of their effect in opening up new markets, or closing existing ones.

"And also the art world kind of passed us by in a way, because one of my friends...when we started at the studio she'd just finished her degree, her MA at Chelsea. There were two of them, they'd done printmaking at Chelsea, and they looked like they were set to do really well, but the kind of work they made again was very materials based, very feeling based, and it was part of the sort of 80s neo-expressionism really. And then the late 80s came, and suddenly it was neo-conceptualism, so they were there, and the art sort of went like that, and bypassed all of us really." (Female, 1990s graduate)

For others, the significance of the 1990s art boom was the opening up of gallery space, particularly in East London. One 1980s graduate describes the time she graduated:

"At the time the whole art scene was in Cork Street then and it was just virtually

impossible to get in to, so you just didn't even bother."

And later:

"After Frieze, it's just been unbelievable really." (Female, 1980s graduate)

Though not all interviewees regard these changes as positive:

"There's been such a culture shift in art education since the 80s, when I did my BA, it was all, you'll just get a studio, and you'll be painting away for 20 years, and you'll be like, if anybody even bothers to knock on your door you'll be so thankful, you'll get a big shock. And then came the Goldsmiths thing…and suddenly it was like, get engaged, and you're a master of your own marketing, and if you haven't made it by the time you're 30 then forget it. So that was just a complete, I suppose it was a kind of Thatcherite translation into, onto artists really." (Female, 1990s graduate)

London in the noughties: different perceptions of how easy it is to work

In the first decade of the 21st century, east London in particular now offers a network of small galleries. As well as offering a shop front to the public, this provides working artists with what they miss most when they work away from London: face-to-face interaction with other artists.

One artist who lives most of her time in Spain explains why she has to return to London for her work:

"Well it's also that I love talking about art and seeing art…and there's so many meetings I have to do. So I only still show in England. And it's constant, when I'm here, it's constant couriers, things going back and forth, so I really, yeah, I need to be here a week of each month." (Female, 1990s graduate)

For those who have moved out of London, maintaining an artistic career is perceived to be more difficult:

"But after a while, you realise that it's all those social connections that you really miss." (Female, 1990s graduate)

"I think it's much easier to make things happen in London, even though there's far

more people there, there's an audience I think there." (Female, 2000s graduate)

"All the galleries in London and obviously all the free galleries in London, when you're an art student, and going in them on a regular basis and seeing the artists' work, talking to them and the galleries and, it was fantastic. The…the second you stop being inside the art world and going to those things you do notice it, I do notice it now." (Female, 1990s graduate)

4.8 Crossover

Many fine artists work in other sectors and influence innovation in them

In assessing crossover – how fine arts graduates influence innovation in the non-fine arts world – we must look at the organisation of artistic labour markets together with their skills and attributes.

One of the complications in assessing this crossover is, as Heinz and Kruger (2001) put it, that "life-course arrangements are becoming more dynamic, less standardised and more self-directed." This clearly applies to our sample, who have had a mix of working experiences. Many have worked in several sectors and occupations (cultural and non-cultural), and maintained a mix of employment and self-employment at different times in their lives.

The survey asks people about their current occupation and reveals that the majority work in the cultural sectors. Just over 40 per cent work primarily in the arts and cultural industries; a further 6 per cent work in publishing and media; and 11 per cent in design, crafts and new media. So, almost 60 per cent of our graduates work in the wider cultural sectors. A further 20 per cent work in education, 4 per cent in health care, with the remainder saying 'other'.[11]

Of the 40 per cent or so of overall respondents with a second job, approximately two in five identify it as being in the arts/cultural industries, 16 per cent education (mainly further and higher education), 8 per cent in health care/medical and 6 per cent in the not-for-profit/charity sector.

The survey can only give us a snapshot of what people are doing at the moment (see Section 4.2 above). But, the interviews allow us to note

11. For full details of this question, see Appendix 2, Q. 26.

how remarkably few fine artists have always only worked in the arts.

Splits between public and private, commercial and not-for-profit arts are less marked in the UK

Markusen *et al.* (2006) look at crossover primarily within the arts and cultural world of the Los Angeles and San Francisco Bay metropolitan areas. We find little evidence that people conceive of the arts world in the terms that their study uses, namely: the commercial sector, the not-for-profit sector and the community sector.[12] This may be because, unlike the US, publicly-funded arts work or galleries in the UK is a larger sector and somewhat different in character from the not-for-profit sector.

Similarly, the split between the commercial and not-for-profit sectors rarely appears so sharp for our graduates – the artists do not distinguish between work they do for the BBC or a commercial channel such as ITV, in terms of ownership or funding structure, for example. Similarly, distinctions between galleries are usually to do with perceptions of quality, not with whether they are publicly or privately owned.

However, public policy work does give artists new audiences, new material and the sense of making a contribution

Where there is some echo of the US findings is in what Markusen *et al.* call the community sector. They argue that this type of work leads artists to a stronger cultural identity and support for integrated social and political activism.

The 'community' sector in the UK does not however correspond very closely to the US model. Much community arts work – as well as 'public policy' work like arts and health – is funded publicly not philanthropically. But artists gain through access to a new audience, a sense of making a political or social contribution, or material that informs their art work. In these ways, their experiences reflect those of the artists studied in Markusen *et al.*'s study. For these artists, the crossover works both ways – their work as artists informs their work in other areas and vice versa.

4.8.1 Cross-fertilisation and crossover from the fine arts to other fields

Employers don't always appreciate fine artists' transferable skills

The question of what fine arts-trained workers bring to other sorts of work is tied closely to the 'transferability' of their skills. Many of our interviewees regard what they have and what they have learned as highly transferable, though some feel that potential employers do not always appreciate this.

In general, our interviewees display a strong sense of pride in their adaptability, which many explicitly link to their educational formation:

> "As I said, the great thing about being an ex-art student is you can live anywhere… You'll turn your hand to any job because you have to, going through art school." (Male, 1960s graduate)

> "It's not a normal way of doing choreography. It, and it comes from my interest, I'm sure, in the visual arts and working from a dynamic or a perceived mood within the image and the tension between these different images and what that means to the performer and how they can translate this into a movement or a, some kind of different dynamic." (Female, 1970s graduate)

> "Which I think is probably why I'm good at it, so, and actually, because actually architects can't do that, because they're too, well, because it's beyond their brief, so it is, so I interact with the architecture, by bringing something much more fluid to it, or if it's very urban, then I bring something that gives you some sense of nature in some way." (Female, 1970s graduate)

The artist can be an interlocutor or 'interpretive' innovator

In some cases, where the link is from the arts to a 'non-arts' world, the respondents see their role as that of an interlocutor. Their descriptions seem to mirror the Lester and Piore description of 'interpretive' innovation, a process of mutual understanding arrived at through exploratory conversations:

> "But I have had a lot of scientists come to the exhibitions and that's because they're interested in how I'm translating their language for other people to access. So I think there's potential for something

12. See Section 2.9 above for a description of these sectors.

to come out of that." (Female, 1990s graduate)

"We have a course on Housing Management, Housing Policy and there's an architecturally based course as well, and I'm about the only teacher who can read across between the two and tries to drag the students back and forth so the architectural students don't ask the right questions about social context and the management ones can't read a plan." (Female, 2000s graduate)

One describes the process of working with a neurologist:

"So, I'd give her a quick run through of everything that I knew and she would just pick up on a few bits. Not quite like that, quite good, and then interpret my knowledge through a visual language. Could we describe it like this? Could we describe it like that? And she'd say no, that's just not right at all and you could describe it like this but there's this, this and this. So through this conversation she would give me the science then I would double back on that science and go, do you mean this? And we ended with a, so then I went away and designed these games." (Female, 1980s graduate)

4.8.2 Cross-fertilisation and crossover from outside the fine arts into the fine arts

Other fields also impact back on the fine arts

The assumption in much of the literature, influenced by David Throsby's work, is that artists use money earned from other work to supplement lack of income from artistic work. They buy time for their practice. There is certainly much evidence for this in our survey and interviews.

We ask people in our survey why they decide to seek employment outside the arts. Given that most respondents either practise primarily in the arts, or consider themselves to be artists, the response rate to this question is surprisingly low. But a third of those who do reply cite the 'need for regular work and income'. Economic reasons are a major factor in taking up other careers. "I was fed up with bar jobs", said one respondent.

What becomes clearer through the interviews, however, is that the skills, ideas and contacts

gained from both arts and non-arts work can be seen as having value:

"I ended up working in a photographic laboratory [in the Ministry of Defence] and getting extremely good technical training for two and a half years." (Female, 1990s graduate)

"And I really enjoyed working on a building site with teams of other kinds of builders, people in the building trade. And it was great just seeing, just being a part of that. They hated us…because really, you're just painting anyway, that's not real work. And we had a lot of sexism, we had quite a lot of racism on the building sites, but it was a great experience. And I think I probably actually learnt to paint there rather than at art school." (Female, 1990s graduate)

"In the surveyors? I think it helps me now still that I had to invoice and I had to chase and I had to negotiate… I even have like a log of my paintings in the same way they had a log of which houses they surveyed. I think it taught me loads." (Female, 1990s graduate)

Few see this cross-fertilisation as problematic; many see it as attractive

Only in a small number of cases is this cross-fertilisation seen as problematic, and this is generally when it is likely to harm their art work:

"I try to avoid any crossover because what I do is really sort of picky work because I work as a sub-editor, it's really kind of close work, and I sometimes worry that that's going to influence my art work and I'm going to end up doing really conservative, really closed art work as well, so I'm trying to avoid that." (Female, 2000s graduate)

For others, reaching out beyond the arts world is the attraction:

"And I think that, that is a real driving force of a lot of the, not the private art we do, but the more interactive public art we do, is getting that kind of buzz back from your audiences." (Female, 1980s graduate)

"We're very much driven by exposing what we think is really exciting art, giving that a platform. Giving it a platform, not only to the art world, which is what a lot of art world stuff just does, it just preaches to the art world, which is fine, but I think

we have a bit of an evangelistic approach that everybody can benefit." (Male, 1980s graduate)

Indeed it can be essential to people's art work

For some, doing other types of more publicly engaged work, or networking outside the arts and cultural industries, is essential to their art work:

"If my only interaction was with those in mine or similar industries I'd have too narrow a spectrum to draw upon when writing and filmmaking." (Male, 1990s graduate)

Those who do not work full-time in the arts also articulate these benefits:

"I think I quite like having different hats on to be honest. I think that's underrated, because if I was a full-time artist I really wouldn't know where to get the ideas from. Because I don't, I can't make art around art, it's, yeah. I've lived that life, at least for a short while and it wasn't very helpful." (Male, 2000s graduate)

Another who works in health care says:

"When I think of the people who were students with me and I think of myself, and I think of my patient group, I think there are quite a lot of parallels so I think understanding from the inside what it feels like to be out of step or not understood or marginalised, and I think art is often difficult for people to understand. So I think there's that sense of being on the edge of something or out of it and misunderstood and I think that's often very useful." (Female, 1960s graduate)

4.8.3 Barriers to crossover – supply

The primary importance attached to being an artist can reduce the willingness to cross over

The overall conclusions of the literature on fine arts graduates are that they generally want to work as artists in their chosen field; they will go to great lengths to do so; and will often move out completely only for financial reasons. In our study, we have also seen that economic reasons are an important factor for those with a career outside the arts and cultural sectors.

However many interviewees regard working as an artist as vocational, not in the sense of a training for a job, but in its more traditional sense as a calling. This Romantic ideal of the values of the artist may have seemed anachronistic in the sixties, let alone the noughties (Frith and Horne, 1987), but it is incredibly persistent. As Frith and Horne argue, the best efforts of industrial pragmatists and cultural studies theorists have not managed to alter the fact that "artists believe in the mystery of individual creation".

Many artists feel they have a calling from an early age

Many of our interviewees describe being interested in art from a very early age – sometimes in the face of parental or school disapproval:

"All the people that I was really fascinated by were artists, and I thought I want to spend my time doing that sort of thing, and hanging out with people like that, and looking like that." (Female graduate, 1970s)

The sense of identification with 'being an artist' is strong, beyond what one might consider a job description:

"So I was kind of at a point where it was like, do I stay being an artist or don't I? But of course that was never really in question, so it was only afterwards I thought, well actually I could have shifted careers if I'd wanted to."

(Interviewer) "But it had never been in question because?"

"Because I was an artist." (Female, 1990s graduate)

'Selling out' is not about making money, but about not being an artist

As Taylor and Littleton (2008) argue in their recent study of art and design graduates, people often use the term 'selling out' in discussions about work and money. This should not be taken as a straightforwardly anti-commercial attitude. They find no evidence that failure to make money is seen as a 'marker' of artistic success, as some commentators have argued (McRobbie, 2002). In our interviews, the term is generally used to describe giving up art work for some other means of making a living; in other words not being an artist.

One who is still working in the arts says:

> "Well the achievement I guess is that I'm still working, I'm not, I'm still not earning much money but I'm still doing really what I want to, I haven't sold out and gone into a full-time office job." (Female, 1990s graduate)

While another, who no longer works as an artist says:

> "I don't think I would have done anything else and I don't think I've 100 per cent given up on being an artist. I'm in this constant, I earn a reasonably good salary now, and I'm very pleased with that and I'd probably say that I earn more than anyone else that I know that did that course. So in that sense I consider myself quite a success, but on the other hand I feel like I've sold out because I don't make art much anymore." (Female, 2000s graduate)

Others seem to feel the need to justify why they are no longer working as an artist:

> "I can't really put all my eggs in one basket and I'm not great at making sacrifice."

And of those on her arts course who do stay in the field, she says:

> "They're quite special and they're quite tough." (Female, 1990s graduate)

And another says of a friend from art school:

> "Because he's been a practising furniture maker, artist all his life, he won't compromise, and he's been very hard up, he's stuck to being an artist." (Female, 1960s graduate)

As discussed below, there is no evidence from our interviews that graduates regard working in other sectors to be 'less creative' than working in the arts, nor do we find any support for the idea that being a commercial success per se is frowned upon. But the desire to be an artist and the importance attached to that, means that people will continue to find ways of working in the arts if possible. In other words, this acts as a primary constraint on crossover.

4.8.4 Barriers to crossover – demand

Employers' failure to recognise artists' transferable skills also acts as a constraint on crossover

For those of our interviewees who have decided in their careers to seek work outside of the arts, a source of frustration is the perceived attitude of employers to those with art school degrees. People describe applying for hundreds of jobs, an experience not uncommon for recent graduates, and having to confront a view that, as one put it, art graduates are 'chaotic'.

For these people, their highly transferable skills are not necessarily recognised by potential employers:

> "I think it's the skills that I learnt at art school that employers overlook when they're looking to employ people, that they suddenly realise are so valuable when they do employ you."

> (Interviewer) "What are they?"

> "And it's that I'm so proactive, that I think for myself. I won't sit there waiting to be told what to do. My nature is to actively solve problems. You have to be so driven and focused as an artist." (Female, 2000s graduate)

Another argued:

> "An employer doesn't, when they interview someone who's recently come out of art school, they see someone who is a maverick, who doesn't necessarily have much rigour." (Male, 2000s graduate)

Part 5: Implications for policy

Our analysis of the literature on the cultural and creative sectors reveals the paucity of research on the role of the fine arts within these sectors. This exposes potential problems with current approaches to policy which lump the cultural and creative industries together.

Recent attempts to study these activities within a policy context have given birth to a variety of classification systems.
The DCMS's thirteen 'creative industry' sectors is one such attempt. Throsby (2001) describes the cultural sectors as a concentric circle model with the arts lying at the centre; a model which has been picked up at European Union (KEA, 2006) and UK policy levels (Andari *et al.*, 2007). This puts the visual arts at the centre of what it describes as 'core arts fields', along with the performing arts and heritage.

We argue that there is a specific need for better understanding of how parts of the cultural and creative industries fit together. Much of the existing research illuminates the patterns of artistic careers, their motivations and the details of their working lives (Frey, 1997; Blackwell and Harvey, 1999; Rengers and Madden, 2000). But the fine arts are generally viewed as a self-contained world, and the literature is rarely linked explicitly to that on the broader culture and creative sectors, let alone innovation.

Better understanding of the different parts of the cultural and creative sectors should illuminate the differences between them, as well as their links. The fine arts labour market is not the same as the labour market for videogames – even though those trained in the fine arts may increasingly work in videogames. It has a different structure, geography and attitude.

However, our interviewees do not describe themselves as being at the centre of a core-periphery model. Although as fine artists, many would be seen as the 'core', they derive ideas and inspiration from other cultural sectors and non-cultural activities. A good example is the way a dance company created a show based on the experience of making short TV programmes. Crossover works in multiple ways.

Artists have the skills to work in other fields
The importance of the arts workforce is not that artistic acts of creation 'precede' other cultural or creative activities. Rather it is that their skills and ways of working equip artists for a wide variety of roles – including a brokerage role within the wider cultural sectors.

The skills of what Lester and Piore (2004) describe as interpretive innovation are strongly reflected in how people describe their working methods.

These skills deserve wider recognition from skills bodies
In many respects, this represents a success for the British art school tradition. But it also presents challenge to skills and education policymakers. The rhetoric of skills bodies sometimes downplays artistic skills in favour of 'business' skills, and suggests that an 'oversupply' of art graduates is a problem.

However, the skills that fine arts students learn – critical thinking, learning by asking around, the ability to understand divergent viewpoints – are also in demand across a range of economic activities. So, skills bodies need to understand them and ensure that they remain a core part of arts education.

We must preserve the best of the old art school in an age of mass higher education

Another challenge for educators is the degree to which the art school education described by many of our interviewees – one based on large amounts of unstructured studio time, with access to tutors and technicians where necessary, and the experience of working alongside other students – is sustainable in an era of mass higher education.

More recent graduates speak of restricted studio space, less access to technicians and of over-crowded courses. A wider range of students, of different ages, may mean less time and opportunity for social interactions. The expansion of higher education is unlikely to be reversed; we need new models of art education that can preserve some of these elements, while serving a wider public.

Policies to encourage crossover should recognise the complexities of artists' careers and the need for artists to maintain their identities

Our study suggests that policies to stimulate crossover – how fine arts graduates contribute to innovation in the wider economy – must recognise the complexity of fine arts graduates' career experiences. They typically work in several sectors and occupations over the course of their working lives (often at the same time), and have maintained a mix of employment and self-employment at different points.

At the same time, policies must also consider the reluctance of fine arts graduates to take up occupations where they cannot identify themselves as artists, or the possibility that employers (and skills agencies) place insufficient weight on their cognitive skills.

Our study also raises possible tensions between the working practices of fine arts graduates which involve a good deal of informal networking – commonly viewed by researchers as conducive to innovation – and attempts to open up artistic labour markets to talent from under-represented communities. This raises significant challenges for policies to increase diversity in the cultural industries.

Policymakers should distinguish between creativity and culture

A final issue is one of language. Policymakers often use culture synonymously with creativity. Creativity is not the particular preserve of artists, as our interviews make clear. It describes a way of working which seems to be highly developed in this workforce, but is by no means exclusive to them. They distinguish their activities with reference to culture not to creativity – to products that essentially communicate meaning, not utility. Nike shoes and cars may contain creative inputs, but one can still go for a run in them or drive. A painting does not have a similar utility function.

The danger of eliding these differences, is not simply that policymakers will fail to communicate with artists, but they will fail to understand what is specific about cultural production and cultural activities. We do not think this is a useful basis for either cultural policy or for innovation policy that seeks to be more informed by the way artists work.

Part 6: Conclusions – fine arts graduates in the UK economy

Our starting point for this research was to investigate the skills and changing work practices of fine arts graduates. We wanted to look at a 50-year period and the extent to which any changes provide a greater understanding of the way fine artists and their skills are being absorbed into the wider economy and what implications this has for innovation.

'Being an artist' remains important across the decades

What is most striking, particularly in the interview data, is the sense of continuity rather than of change. There is a consistency across the decades in the reasons for wanting to study art; the benefits of an art school education; attitudes to skills and capabilities learned; and the importance attached to working as an artist.

This is not to deny that things have changed. Contemporary art school students are educated in a mass higher education system, with many more students and less physical space. The growth of the visual arts market means that they are more likely than their predecessors to see being an artist as a possible career; yet they know that despite the importance attached to celebrity, they have no more guarantee of 'making it' than their predecessors had. But in their attitudes towards the importance and desirability of 'being an artist' we find relative little change.

This is important because it helps to inform some of the contemporary debate about cultural workers (Ross, 2003; Neff, 2005), and the degree to which artists seem to combine a precarious and economically insecure existence with joy and pleasure in their work (Gill, 2007). To such pleasure, we would add a perceived ethical importance among our respondents in working as an artist.

Three ways in which artistic labour is absorbed in the overall economy

So, how do the arts contribute to innovation? We have identified three possible mechanisms by which artistic labour is absorbed in the overall economy.

1. Interpretive innovation – experimental skills and an openness to new ideas

The first is that the skills that artistically trained workers bring are an important element of 'interpretive' innovation (Lester and Piore, 2004). We find considerable support for this from our interviewees. Many respondents give examples of divergent thinking, or the ability to see things from multiple viewpoints. In work across disciplinary boundaries, fine arts graduates will often see themselves as brokers or interpreters.

There is a strong perception that the traditional art school education, with its emphasis on self-discovery, unstructured learning and the social processes of working with other students in a studio are in part responsible for the development of these particular skills.

As it is not the aim of this work to quantify innovation, we cannot say that these skills are responsible for any particular amount of innovation. But the process described is very close to that identified in other research as an important component of innovation.

2. Networked structures and informal labour foster innovation

The second mechanism is that artistic labour is organised in such a way that it offers a prototype for other forms of work (as well as less desirable facets such as unpaid work). Although many of our respondents are currently self-employed, networked structures are important, particularly in processes of innovation and change, where social and professional connections are often the way in which these changes are realised.

3. Creative inputs are an important part of everyday products, though artists distinguish between symbolic (cultural) and utilitarian production

The third argument is that not only have the cultural sectors themselves expanded, but that creative inputs have become a part of almost all production from cars to airport terminals. The expansion of cultural markets has clearly opened up opportunities for fine arts graduates in everything from pop music video to urban regeneration.

However, our respondents continue to distinguish between the arts and culture and other 'creative outputs' (such as cars or running shoes), a distinction not always made by some policymakers and academics. The distinction between symbolic (cultural) and utilitarian production remains relevant to fine artists. This is something which has implications for wide-ranging notions like the 'creative industries', and for policies which aim to stimulate the links between them and innovation in the wider economy.

The survey and interviews show that interaction across sectors is commonplace. Even though almost 60 per cent of our sample work primarily in the arts and cultural industries, the networked nature of the arts market and the need to supplement income at various times by multiple job-holding, ensures that fine arts graduates often work beyond the boundaries of their specialism. They are to be found using arts in urban regeneration schemes, collaborating with scientists, or working at second jobs from construction to education. Crossover between artists and other parts of the economy is a characteristic at some point in most artists' working lives.

Appendix 1: Research methodology

Sample

For this project, the research team negotiated unique access to a previously unused database of University of the Arts London (UAL) alumni who have studied fine arts at one of the University's constituent colleges. The database included those who have studied painting, sculpture, fine art photography, fine art, film and video or combined arts as undergraduates or postgraduates.

Fine arts was chosen both as a 'core' educational stage for practising artists and the most 'abstract' part of the art school syllabus. While one might reasonably expect those who study design to pursue careers in design, or those who study fashion to enter the fashion industry (or related areas like retailing), the less obviously 'vocational' nature of a fine arts education made it easier to focus on the core skills base. Choosing fine arts as opposed to 'all the subjects that arts schools teach', meant that our sample had a common educational basis, allowing us to define which UAL graduates we surveyed.

Using UAL alumni allowed us access to a major data resource that would have otherwise been impossible to construct. In doing so, however, we were not proposing the UAL as a 'typical' art school. Its elite status and its location within London are both positive attractions for students and determinants of the kind of students it produces; though it should be noted that many of our respondents have also attended other art colleges in the UK and elsewhere, either for foundation or undergraduate studies.

Online survey

We used an online survey for several reasons, among them speed of response and relative ease of collation.

There is some evidence (Markusen, Gilmore, Johnson, Levi and Martinez, 2006) that response rates for online surveys are higher than for postal surveys and yield longer and more original answers to qualitative questions. A telephone survey is more costly, and does not allow the respondents to answer 'in their own time'. We were initially worried that we might not reach as many older respondents, or that they may be less willing to fill in an online survey; but these concerns proved to be unfounded.

Online surveys enable more answer options, permit more interaction and facilitate skip patterns with questions; all are particularly useful for a complex, biographical approach. In addition, online surveys facilitate digital coding of the data.

The survey was initially emailed to 8,000 addresses via the alumni association. We anticipated that this route would engender greater 'buy-in' and help boost response rates. We had a 6.4 per cent response rate.

Importantly, when we asked online respondents if they were willing to be interviewed in person for further research, 67 per cent agreed. This reinforces the value of the initial survey, and the subsequent methodology, as it enabled us to access a sample of people who had already 'bought in' to the process and thus were willing to invest the time and effort needed in recalling biographical detail.

In order to understand the particular characteristics of our survey sample better, we also drew up an abridged survey, focussing on key characteristics, which we posted on the A-N newsletter/artists information site (www.a-n.co.uk), the Artquest website and on NESTA's website. This functioned as a sort of 'health check' on our survey, helping us to see if its characteristics were broadly in line with other art school graduates.

We received 115 responses to the abridged survey, with graduates coming from a wide variety (some 56) of colleges. The sample was somewhat younger than our original sample: 70 per cent had graduated since 2000 (as opposed to just over half in the original sample). In addition, women outnumbered men by an even greater margin in the second sample – 82 per cent of follow-up respondents were female. Given that members of Artquest and readers of A-N newsletter are likely to be practising artists (93 per cent described themselves thus), over 60 per cent of the respondents to the follow-up survey worked primarily in the arts and cultural industries, as opposed to 40 per cent of the original sample; and only 7 per cent of the sample worked in education.

Beyond this, however, the follow up sample largely reflected the original sample. The numbers who consider networking important, both within and outside the arts sectors were similar at around 40 per cent and 30 per cent respectively . In both cases, around 44 per cent were self-employed and had set up a business, and the form of artistic work was also similar; while 37 per cent of our original sample were painters, 32 per cent of the follow-up sample also described themselves in this way. For a full description of the second survey results, see Appendix 3.

Work biography interviews

Of the respondents willing to be interviewed, we eliminated overseas residents, for reasons of cost and practicality. From the rest, we constructed a sample which focused on key characteristics that we wished to investigate, based on the literature review.

We thus drew up the sample of interviewees to achieve a quota of 40, which represented a balance of:

- **Decade of graduation** – to explore changes that have occurred and get a good mix of ages.

- **Gender** – the majority of questionnaire respondents were women and this was reflected in the interviews. It also allowed us to explore any gender-related issues.

- **Working primarily as an artist/not as an artist** (embedded versus specialised). Other NESTA research (Higgs, Cunningham and Bakhshi, 2008) has argued that 'creatives' are increasingly employed outside the cultural and creative sectors. We wanted to see if that was the case with our graduates – to explore what lies behind that in terms of motivation and what impact, if any, this has had on innovation in the wider economy.

- **Geography** – in this case we had two 'categories': those working inside London; and those in the rest of the UK. This enabled us to explore the 'London' factor and the extent to which working outside the capital may affect practising artists.

- **A mix of those working primarily with others and those working alone** – enabling us fully to explore the issues around collaboration.

Our interview sample was not intended to be statistically representative of those completing the online questionnaire, nor of the UAL fine arts alumni population. There were a number of practical issues which we sought to control for:

- The majority of respondents had graduated since 2000, so we 'over sampled' those from previous decades to achieve a better mix of ages and get more extensive biographies.

- There were more painters than any other group (37 per cent of those who replied re: primary artistic practice), so we over-sampled those who work primarily in other media, to get a better mix and to pick up differences in changing technology and links to other sub-sectors.

- The majority of respondents work at least some of the time as artists. We had many of these in the sample, but we also wanted to investigate how fine artists contribute to innovation in other cultural sectors. We thus over-sampled those who work in fields such as film and TV, theatre or music.

By adopting a biographical approach we have been able to contextualise our graduates and examine other issues, derived from the literature review. These include patterns of formal and informal learning and the attitudes that promote innovation, including resilience, risk-taking and a willingness to learn.

Biographical approaches can explore people "situated within everyday life" (Halfacree and Boyle, 1993: 338), rather than abstracted as static members of occupational groups or socio-economic types. It obviously involves questions of both 'life' and 'work' and the blurring of boundaries and the dynamic relationship between the two (Jarvis and Pratt, 2006). As Heinz and Kruger (2001) argue, it also plays on traditional sociological concerns about the relationship between social structure and personal agency.

Based on the recent literature about artists at work (Throsby and Hollister, 2003), both of these issues are acute when considering research with artists (and, no doubt, other groups). For some, the notion of being an artist is meant to dissolve the work-leisure distinction. At the same time, the Romantic ideology of many of the artists meant that interviewees often place great stress on personal agency – the notion of being outside, or even opposed to 'the system' remains one that resonates in various way with this group (Frith and Horne, 1987). Hence the importance of using an appropriate research tool sensitive to these factors. By using 'turning points' and significant biographical events, we hope to get beneath simple description to see how both personal agency and institutional structures help to determine changes and outcomes.

Analysis

The interviews were taped, transcribed and then analysed using content analysis software, ATLAS.ti. The interviews were marked up and coded, and the software made searching and comparison easier, which was vital as the total interview material amounted to almost 400,000 words.

Qualitative coding, the process of defining the interview data, was the first analytic step. It meant naming segments of interview transcript with labels that simultaneously categorised, summarised and accounted for them. We created these codes by defining what we see in the data. The same notions were referred to by different respondents, and the codes were thus refined into themes.

The process was highly interactive and transcripts were read many times for meaning. It also allowed us to construct and compare 'families' of respondents, such as gender or decade of graduation, to see if there were any 'family' resemblances.

It should be emphasised however that, despite relatively sophisticated software, analysing qualitative data is an essentially interpretive task. As Charmaz (2006: 43) puts it: "We aim to make an interpretative rendering that begins with coding and illuminates studied life".

Appendix 2: Full survey results

Q. 1 What University of the Arts College(s) did you graduate from?

Percentage of respondents

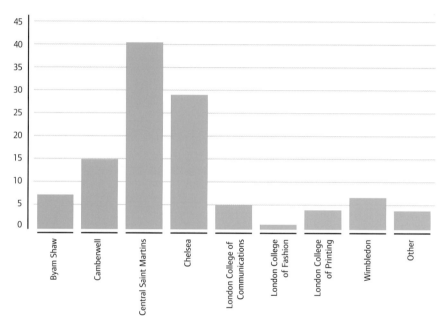

Answered: 494 out of 508

Q. 2 When did you graduate?

Percentage of respondents

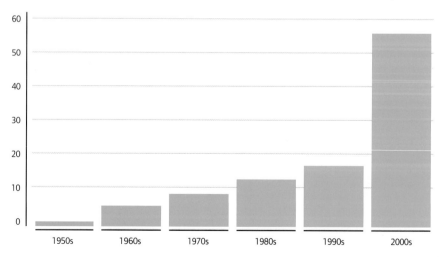

Answered: 486 out of 508

Q. 3 What fine arts qualification(s) were you awarded by your college?

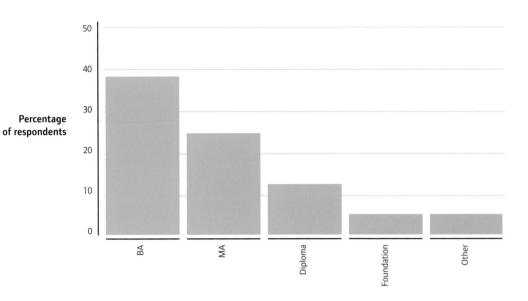

Answered: 474 out of 508

Q. 4 What qualification(s) did you have before you started your fine arts course?

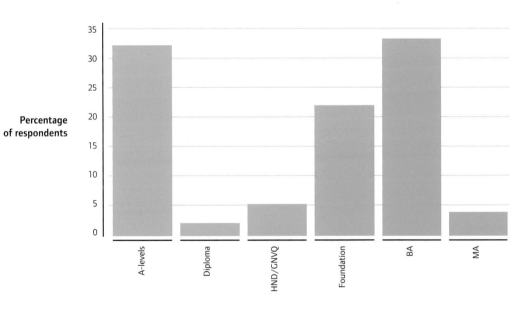

Answered: 381 out of 508

Q. 5 What qualification(s) have you gained since leaving UAL?

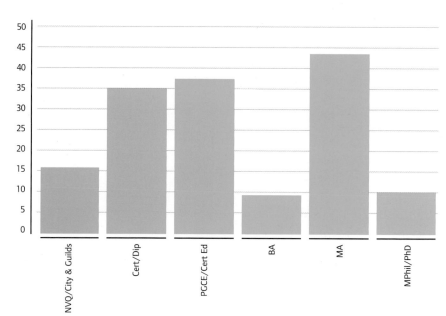

Percentage of respondents

Answered: 260 out of 508

Q. 6 Have you received formal training or course of instruction after completing your Fine Arts studies?

Yes: 44 per cent
No: 56 per cent

Answered: 433 out of 508

Q. 7 In which area(s) was this (formal) training? Please select all that apply.

Top three answers selected:

1. 2D fine art – e.g. drawing, painting, print, photo-media (24 per cent)

2. Fine art digital media/photography and design applications – CAD, Flash, Maya, Photoshop, etc. (22 per cent each)

3. ICT/IT (16 per cent)

Respondents selected from 14 categories of training and were invited to write in any applicable training not listed. About half of the respondents selected 'Other' and provided write-in answers. Of these, two areas of training stand out: 13 per cent of respondents have received teacher training or other instruction in teaching/education and just under 9 per cent have trained in mental health or counselling (including psychotherapy and cognitive analysis).

Answered: 433 out of 508

What prompted you to attend this training and how was it funded (e.g. self-funded, subsidised by employer, government grant or other?)[13]

Over 50 per cent of respondents were self-funded, and just over 30 per cent have been funded by an employer. Only around 17 per cent of respondents have received public funding.

The reasons for undertaking further formal education are, as expected, varied but many can be categorised as continuing professional development. One respondent speaks of "the desire to learn a practical skill to use my creativity in a commercial way", while another speaks of learning new technical skills "to turn my fine arts works into products".

Respondents also show a strong streak of non-instrumental learning: the desire to know more about a subject for professional and personal satisfaction. One is a strong advocate of continuing education, another spoke of studying anthropology, "because I wanted to study wider social issues and expand my mind". Others are however more basic: "I need money to eat food and pay rent."

Answered: 163 out of 508

Q. 9 Which training was most useful and how did you benefit from it?

Most respondents have used postgraduate training either to develop further avenues for 'professional' work or to change career or career direction substantially. IT courses, including web design, Dreamweaver and HTML are regarded as particularly useful. "I wish I had known this earlier" is a typical comment, though these experiences are more common for those who have graduated more than ten years ago (and therefore were less likely to have been exposed to IT as part of formal education).

Others completed teacher training such as PGCE courses and have moved into art education, though many of them continue to practise as artists.

Answered: 141 out of 508

13. 'This training' refers to formal training after fine arts degree.

Q. 10 Have you participated in informal learning after completing your degree(s)? This includes on-the-job training, using books and references, self-teaching, and observing co-workers or members of a studio or collective.

Yes: 80 per cent
No: 20 per cent

Across five decades of graduates, the percentage remains relatively stable, at around 80 per cent; fine arts graduates from the 1980s have the highest percentage of informal training, with 87 per cent reporting participation. Respondents whose primary job is in the arts/cultural industries also report 87 per cent participation.

Answered: 407 out of 508

Q. 11 Please describe this informal learning: what prompted you to undertake it and how was it funded or supported?

The vast majority of respondents have continued to undertake a wide variety of informal learning. Indeed, the interest in learning and willingness to undertake it is striking. "Informal learning has been critical to my desire to progress," says one, while another says: "You should never stop learning. It's a sin!"

The majority use a mix of informal learning methods. The following typical response sums up the variety of ways in which those working primarily as artists continue to learn and improve their practice: "reading books, talking to friends, associates and former tutors, attending lectures and private views".

On-the-job learning is common, whether the job is inside the cultural sectors or outside. "Sculpture is about problem solving," says one, "and every piece of work has had an element of self-learning". Those who are working in other cultural sectors, such as TV or film, also tend to describe on-the-job learning as the primary way in which they have learned about a new industry or become 'embedded'.

A notable point about informal (and indeed formal) learning is that it is often unpaid – with artists bearing the financial costs of learning and career changes themselves. This reflects other recent work, suggesting that this is a common pattern in the cultural sectors.[14]

Answered: 276 out of 508

14. See for example Randle, K. and Culkin, N. (2007) 'Getting in and getting on in Hollywood: Freelance careers in an uncertain industry.' Paper presented at the Expert Seminar on Precarious Labour in the E Society, LSE, March 2007; a similar finding is reported in the Crossover study, Markusen, *et al.* (2006).

Q. 12 What skills have you learned from your fine arts education? Please select all that apply.

Two-thirds of the total survey respondents answered this question.

Top three answers selected:

1. Work independently with self-motivation (84 per cent)

2. Analytical and critical reasoning (82 per cent)

3. Aesthetic appreciation (79 per cent)

Other popular answer choices included 'Theoretical skills' – the ability to put your work into context (74 per cent) and 'Create original works' (73 per cent). The ability to work constructively with others and technical fine arts skills were also selected by more than 50 per cent of the respondents.

Write-in responses may be broadly grouped into two areas: 'self-belief and confidence' and 'networking.' One graduate summed up the skills learned as being "largely about confidence…the ability to say 'I am an artist' rather than 'I like to draw'".

More recent graduates select 'Analytical and critical reasoning' or 'Aesthetic appreciation' as the skills they have learned from studying fine arts. 'Theoretical skills' is the second most popular skill chosen by most recent graduates (2000-07), who rank it higher than 'Aesthetic appreciation'.

Eighty-six per cent of respondents working in the arts/cultural industries say they learned to 'Work independently with self-motivation' (the top response for this category).

Answered: 348 out of 508

Q. 13 What is the most important thing that you have learned from studying fine arts, and how has it influenced your professional life? This may include subject matter, curriculum and/or experiences outside the classroom.

Very few respondents cite technical skills as the most important thing they have learned, instead focusing on cognitive, or soft skills. As the question is a 'write-in', people often express similar notions in different ways, but over 16 per cent mention 'critical thinking' as the most important thing they have learned.

Most are grateful for their time at art school, though there are some criticisms that it did not prepare them fully for life outside. "College did not teach me much", says one, "although having had access to the Life Room has been invaluable throughout my career". Another recalls that when they studied there were few attempts to teach students about life after graduation, though it is "different now".

For art students, as for other beneficiaries of higher education, the socialising experience counts as much as formal education: "the change of scene, becoming independent and sharing a big house with strangers informed my development as a person, and therefore as an artist far more than any syllabus could have".

Answered: 317 out of 508

Q. 14 What advice would you give to fine arts students starting their educational career today?

There is a lot of advice about self-management – much of it exhortations to focus, work hard and believe in yourself. There is an interesting split in respondents between those who advise students to focus more on practical issues concerned with future employment, and those whose advice is to concentrate on internal motivations. "Don't think in terms of career", says one, and another advises "don't follow trends, follow your heart – ignore fashion, branding and the marketplace".

Others suggest more of an external focus would be of benefit. Many advise doing other training such as a PGCE, a creative writing course, business management or IT skills. Indeed, around a third of respondents advise doing some other formal education alongside a degree in fine arts.

Concerns about the financial viability of a career as an artist lead some respondents to say their advice to fine arts students would be 'don't'. Indeed social and economic distinctions between respondents may play a role here as several respondents draw attention to the difficulty of earning a living in the arts world without the support of a high parental income. "Unless you have money behind you it is very difficult to make a living."

Answered: 311 out of 508

Q. 15 What is your current or most recent job title?

As there are no length restrictions to the answers to this write-in question, it is not uncommon for respondents to describe what they do rather than list a specific job title: "I am a self-employed artist" or "I am way past retirement age but work voluntarily as a teacher of English to local Bengali women", and "I have been leading a dual-role lifestyle: artist and project director (voluntary basis), and information officer (publications)". How people define themselves is also reflected by the fact that almost 15 per cent of respondents write compound job titles, most of which include some type of artistic practice, for example 'artist, facilitator, production assistant', and 'painter/writer/illustrator'. Just under 30 per cent of respondents consider themselves a full- or part-time artist or designer, with some defining themselves by medium: 'glass artist' or 'installation artist'.

Answered: 326 out of 508

Q. 16 What is your current employment status?

Almost 70 per cent of respondents are either 'Employed full-time' (24 per cent); 'Employed part-time' (18 per cent); or 'Self-employed on a long-term contract' (29 per cent). The next highest response rate is for 'Self-employed on a short-term contract' (12 per cent). Six per cent of respondents say they are unemployed while others are on maternity leave, sabbatical, retired or studying. The write-in responses mainly consist of combinations of categories such as 'self-employment and PAYE'. At least one respondent articulates her artistic practice and primary occupation in independent terms, as she put it: "self-employed as therapist and unemployed as artist".

Answered: 342 out of 508

Q. 17-25 Retirees

These questions are answered only by retirees and seek similar information to those asked of non-retirees (see below). Only seven of the 508 respondents define themselves as retired. However, additional respondents consider themselves semi-retired, retired from work but still practising as an artist, and/or work on a voluntary basis; this becomes clear from analysing write-in responses and is reflected in the individual question summaries below.

Of the seven retirees, three have retired from a career in secondary or higher education and one retired from the health care/medical and leisure, food service or hospitality sectors. Six of the seven retirees have worked at least one second job, and these are divided between five sectors: design, education, health care, publishing/media and not-for-profit/charity.

When asked "Have you ever considered yourself a practising artist?", 43 per cent of the retirees say "Yes". Just one selects the answer choice "Yes, but I am no longer a practising artist", highlighting that many fine arts graduates of retirement age do not see themselves as retired even though they no longer engage in paid work, by virtue of the fact that they still practise art.

Answered: 7 out of 508

Q. 26 In which sector is your primary occupation?

Almost 70 per cent of respondents are either 'Employed full-time' (24 per cent); 'Employed part-time' (18 per cent). Unlike Q. 15, where respondents are asked to write in their current or most recent job title(s), this question provides 17 answer choices/job sectors to choose from including 'Other' with a write-in provision. Approximately 90 per cent of respondents to this question choose a sector from the answers provided.

Arts/Cultural industries	40.4 per cent
Architecture/Engineering	1.8 per cent
Design	4.3 per cent
New media	3.2 per cent
Crafts/Applied arts—including ceramics and metalworking	3.5 per cent
Communications/Telecommunications	0.4 per cent
Computing/IT	2.1 per cent
Education – early childhood	0.0 per cent
Education – primary or secondary	6.4 per cent
Education – further or higher	13.8 per cent
Health care/Medical	4.3 per cent
Leisure, Food Service, Hospitality	1.4 per cent
Manufacturing	0.4 per cent
Publishing/Media	6.0 per cent
Not-for-profit/Charity	0.4 per cent
Retail	2.8 per cent
Science and Technology	0.0 per cent
Other (please specify)	8.8 per cent
Answered: 282 out of 508	**100 per cent**

Q. 27 Why did you seek primary employment outside the arts?

The "need for regular work and income" sums up just over a third of responses to this question. It is clear that economic reasons were a major factor in taking up other careers: "I was fed up with bar jobs", says one. However, those who work in the wider cultural industries (film, TV, design) or in art education still consider themselves to be working in the arts.

Others see it as primarily a way to support their work in the arts, but only a small number see working in the non-arts world as a positive chance to explore other opportunities.

Answered: 98 out of 508

Q. 28 Are you a member of any professional associations? If yes, which one(s) and how has membership influenced you work?

Seventy-five per cent of respondents answering this question and who are working in the arts/cultural industries, are (or have been) members of associations/ organisations. The majority of these are members of studios/collectives, and (to a lesser degree) the artists' network.

For those who work outside the arts, about half are members of professional organisations and about half are not. Professionals associations mentioned include teachers and journalists' unions, psychotherapy groups, commercial organisations, such as Chambers of Commerce, and interest groups.

Answered: 65 out of 508

Q. 29 Which factors were/are important in advancing your professional development? Please select all that apply.

The majority of respondents select multiple factors.

Top three answers:

1. Self-motivation (92 per cent)

2. University or art college education (74 per cent)

3. Willingness to change or try new things (76 per cent)

The only other factors to receive more than 50 per cent of votes are 'Experience' (72 per cent) and 'Natural talent/ability' (70 per cent). More than 40 per cent of respondents cite support from peers, colleagues, family and friends as advancing professional development. There is also an indication that chance, or being in the right place at the right time, is important as almost one third (32 per cent) select 'a lucky break' and 'financial support at an important time in my career'.

The top answers for respondents whose primary job is in the arts/cultural industries are 'Experience' and 'Opportunities to exhibit' (79 per cent each) followed by 'Natural talent' (75 per cent), 'Access to studio' and 'University or art college education' (72 per cent each).

Answered: 106 out of 508

Q. 30 What factors have inhibited your professional development at any time in your career?

Compared with the previous question, the responses to this question are more evenly distributed amongst the answer choices. Financial investment and return is the most common factor.

Top three answers:

1. Lack of financial return (55 per cent)

2. Lack of capital to invest in business/equipment/workspace (38 per cent)

3. Domestic responsibilities (35 per cent)

Twenty-two per cent cite lack of funds for further education/training as having a negative effect on professional development and 22 per cent say that their professional development has not been inhibited at any time.

Unsurprisingly, a much higher percentage of female (42 per cent) than male respondents (18 per cent) say that domestic responsibilities inhibited their professional development. Women are also more likely to cite lack of capital to invest in a business or workspace and lack of funding for further education or training.

Looking at graduates by decade, the percentage of those who say their development has not been inhibited in any way falls steadily, from 50 per cent of 1960s graduates, to 27 percent of 1980s graduates, and finally, 10 per cent of most recent graduates (2000-07).

Answered: 103 out of 508

Q. 31 In addition to your primary occupation, do you hold a second job?

Yes: 39 per cent
No: 61 per cent

Answered: 278 out of 508

Q. 32 Which sector is your second job in?

Of the 39 per cent of overall respondents who say they have a second job, 39 per cent identify it as being in the arts/cultural industries. Sixteen per cent work in 'Education' (the majority in higher or further ed), 8 per cent in 'Health care/ Medical' and 6 per cent in the 'Not-for-profit/charity sector'.

Answered: 107 out of 508

Q. 33 Have you ever considered yourself a practising artist?

Yes: 87 per cent
No: 13 per cent

Answered: 329 out of 508

Q. 34 What is (or was) your primary artistic practice?

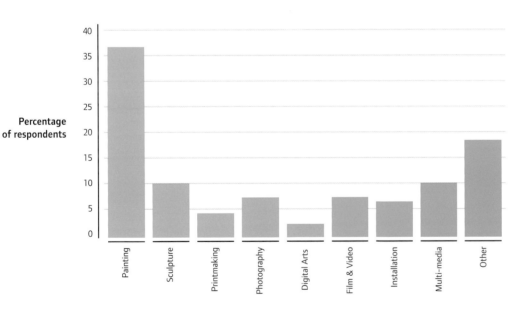

Percentage of respondents

Answered: 284 out of 508

Q. 35 How do you find or begin artistic projects/work? Please select all that apply?

This question presents a list of 15 answer choices, each of which is selected by at least 10 per cent of respondents. The vast majority of artists (89 per cent) say they "undertake self-initiated work". This is followed by a number of ways of finding artistic work which all receive 30 per cent of responses or more: 'Networking' (47 per cent); 'Undertake work commissioned by private individuals (37 per cent); 'Offered direct work' (36 per cent); 'Raise funds to realise my own projects' (31 per cent); 'Apply for grants' (30 per cent).

Fourteen per cent say that they pay to advertise their artistic services/practice, and 28 per cent find work through an agency, gallery or dealer.

Q. 36 How do you promote your artistic projects or work? Please select all that apply.

Seventy-three per cent promote artistic work through exhibitions, followed by 'Self-promotion' (71 per cent) and 'Word of mouth' (64 per cent). Approximately 42 per cent promote projects on website(s), either their own or those run by others. Approximately one-third of respondents promote their work through an agency or gallery, memberships in arts organisations, and by appearing at events, festivals and competitions. The lowest response rate is for promotion via 'Retail spaces', which receives fewer than 3 per cent of votes.

Q. 37 Which best describes the working style of your primary artistic practice?

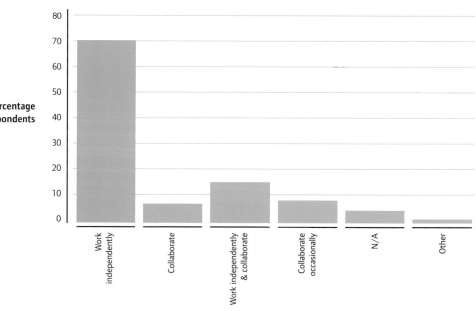

Answered: 283 out of 508

Q. 38 Are you or have you ever been a member of any artists' organisations, studios or collectives?

Yes: 64 per cent
No: 36 per cent

Answered: 283 out of 508

Which artists' organisations, studios and/or collectives do you belong to or have you previously belonged to and how have they influenced your work?

For most respondents, membership is less about influencing their actual work than about providing social or networking opportunities. "A good chance to meet and talk to like-minded people" is a typical response.

Membership is perceived to influence work through motivation, professional support and inspiration rather than a change in technique, practice or access to a new market. Indeed some are resistant to the notion that being a member of a group has influenced them – "they haven't, I hope" is one response to the influence question.

The emotional support given by studios and informal collectives is mentioned by several respondents. "It was a great way to start working and support each other, it gave strength to the artists", says one.

Answered: 165 out of 508

Q. 40 Which stage are you at in your life as a practising artist?

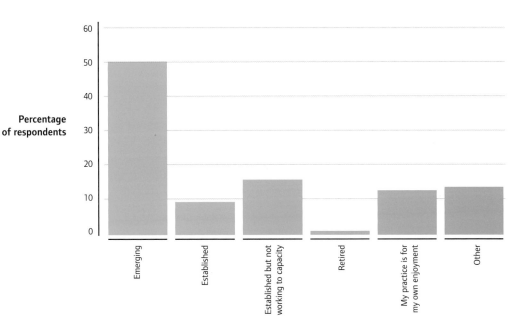

Percentage of respondents

Answered: 282 out of 508

Q. 41 What do you consider to be the key moments of establishment in your life as an artist?

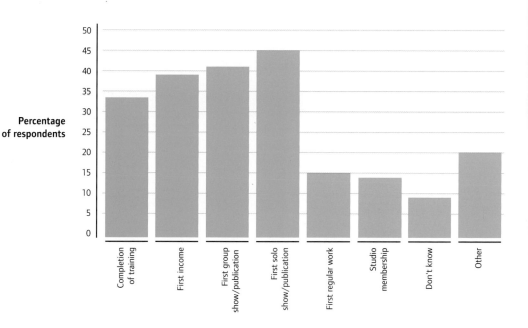

Percentage of respondents

Respondents to this question are able to select more than one answer. Of those who select 'Other', sample write-in answers include having work included in public collections, receiving regular commissions, and specific achievements such as being "Chosen for bursary by the Royal British Society of Sculptors" or having a "Sold out print at the R[oyal] A[cademy]."

Answered: 281 out of 508

Q. 42 Which factors were/are important in advancing your artistic career?

Four of the 23 answer choices are selected by over 70 per cent of respondents: 'University/art college education' (73 per cent); 'Experience' (74 per cent); 'Natural talent' (73 per cent); 'Opportunities to exhibit work' (74 per cent). 'Manual training/skill in artistic practice' is important to almost 60 per cent, as is support from peers, colleagues and fellow students. Forty-seven per cent of respondents say that support from family and friends has been important.

Financial factors, including support at an important time in one's career, receipt of a grant or study grant and participation in an allowance scheme are all chosen by at least 25 per cent of respondents.

The lowest scoring choices are support from an employer, and support from a union or professional organisation, with less than 10 per cent each. Just 8 per cent opt to write-in an answer; the majority of those who do list self-motivation as important in advancing their artistic career.

Answered: 276 out of 508

Q. 43 What factors have inhibited your artistic development at any time in your life?

Ninety-one per cent of respondents believe that their artistic development has been inhibited, primarily by financial factors. The most popular answer choice is lack of financial return (58 per cent), followed by lack of capital to invest in materials/equipment/workspace (45 per cent).

Three additional answers are selected by approximately 40 per cent of respondents: 'Financial constraints restricting opportunities to exhibit'; 'No access to studio or workspace'; and 'Lack of time due to domestic responsibilities'. The lowest response rate is for 'Lack of avenues for publicising work or talent' (14 per cent).

Answered: 276 out of 508

Q. 44 What were your sources of encouragement, support or motivation for studying fine arts?

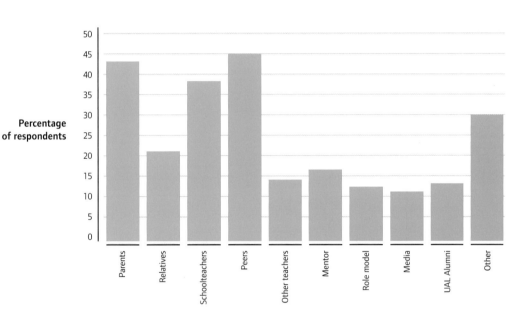

Answered: 319 out of 508

Q. 45 What were your sources of discouragement for studying fine arts?

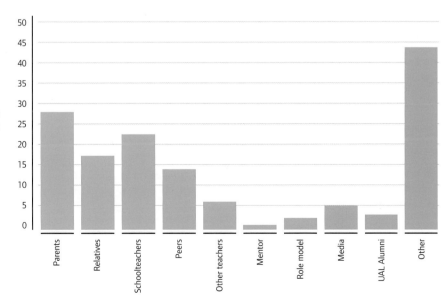

A relatively high percentage of respondents (43 per cent) cite 'other' sources of discouragement. Over 70 per cent of those writing in say they have not been discouraged to study fine arts by anyone or anything. Eight per cent are discouraged by a perceived financial disadvantage to studying fine arts, for example, "Knowing not being able to make a living" and "Lack of money in the field" are two responses. A small number write in that friends or partners have discouraged them.

Answered: 320 out of 508

Q. **46** Was/is one or both of your parents/caregivers an artist?

Yes, one: 18 per cent
Yes, both: 5 per cent
No: 77 per cent

Answered: 301 out of 508

Q. **47** Have you experienced one or more periods without paid work?

Yes: 81 per cent
No: 19 per cent

Answered: 319 out of 508

Q. **48** Why were you without paid work? Please select all that apply.

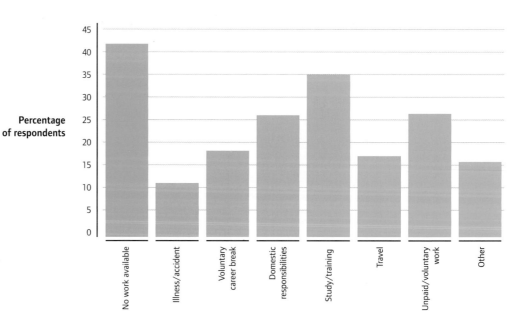

Sixteen per cent of respondents to this question select 'other' and write in an answer; of these, nearly one third say they were without paid work in order to have more time to practise their art. For example, "I was too busy making art" and "Investing time in studio practice" are two of the responses.

Answered: 258 out of 508

Q. 49 Have you ever been supported by unemployment benefits (this includes participation in an enterprise allowance scheme)?

Yes, once: 27 per cent
Yes, more than once: 23 per cent
No: 50 per cent

Answered: 301 out of 508

Q. 50 How did a voluntary career break affect your primary artistic occupation?

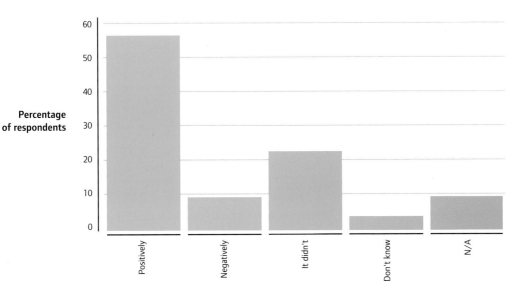

Answered: 32 out of 508

Q. 51 How important is/was networking and social interaction with fine artists and others in the cultural industries to you and your career?

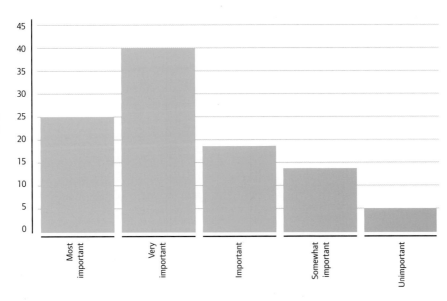

Respondents working primarily in the arts/cultural industries are among the highest sub-category of respondents to rank networking and social interaction within these industries to be important; just 11 per cent consider it to be only somewhat important or unimportant.

Answered: 312 out of 508

Q. 52 How important is/was networking and social interaction with others outside of the arts and cultural industries to you and your career?

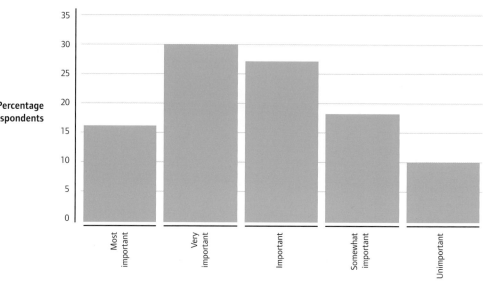

Percentage of respondents

Seventy-three per cent of those working in the arts/cultural industries consider networking outside these industries as Most Important, Very Important, or Important.

Answered: 312 out of 508

Q. 53 At any point in your career, have intellectual property issues been relevant to your work?

Yes: 40 per cent
No: 47 per cent
Don't know: 13 per cent

Forty per cent of respondents to this question say that intellectual property issues have been relevant to their work. Of these, 72 per cent provide an explanation; the most common ways in which artists have worked with IP issues is in the context of royalties and copyright related to published works and the reproduction of images. As one commercial photographer explains: "I am a photographer and graphic designer represented by several galleries and on-line agencies who work with corporate clients. They don't work with you unless your work is copyrighted and IP cleared".

Artists also engage with IP issues in terms of the technical aspects or conceptual nature of their work – "by using copyrighted, images in my work" – or as another artist notes, "conceptually, through the use of old commercial amateur photographic imagery in my own work".

Graduates from the 1990s are the most likely to consider IP issues to be relevant to their work, with 63 per cent answering Yes, as compared with 37 per cent of those graduating during the 1980s and 33 per cent from the 2000s.

Almost one-half of those working in the arts/cultural industries consider IP issues relevant to their work, 6 per cent higher than the overall average.

Answered: 312 out of 508

Q. 54 Have you ever set up a business?

Yes: 45 per cent
No: 55 per cent

Answered: 313 out of 508

Q. 55 When you set up your business, what advice and funding (if any) did you receive and from whom?

Around a third (35 per cent) say they have received no advice at all and around 44 per cent have received no funding. Of those who have received some funding help, 18 per cent have benefited from public funding of some sort including the Enterprise Allowance Scheme, Arts Council grants or money from the Princes' Youth Business trust. Around 14 per cent have had financial help from their family and the same percentage have received bank loans.

Advice came from family and friends; and from accountants or banks.

Q. 56 How did you think setting up a business would benefit you?

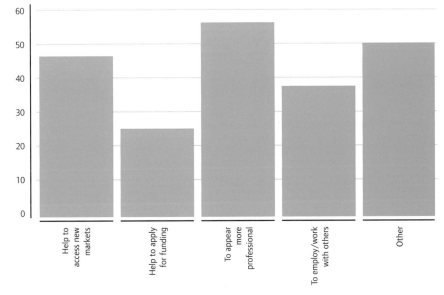

Of the 50 per cent who answered 'other', almost one third thought that setting up a business would have helped to 'support myself' or 'be independent'. Another third believed that a business would have brought tax benefits or enabled them to make more money.

Answered: 96 out of 508

Q. 57 How do you see your future employment?

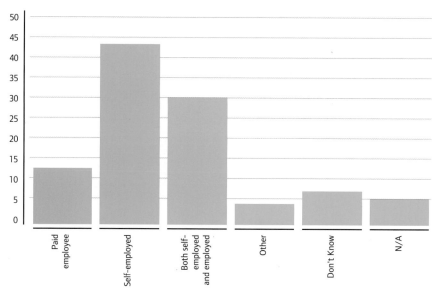

Percentage of respondents

Answered: 308 out of 508

15. A similar finding is reported in the Crossover study, Markusen *et al.* (2006).

Q. 58 Could you provide an example of where working in one sector has led to work in another sector, or changed the nature of your work in another sector?

Many respondents' give examples of moving from one sort of activity to another – particularly between art practice, teaching and voluntary work.

In some cases, working for charities or doing voluntary work has led directly to work in the third sector or to an interest in therapy of various kinds.

On respondent argues that: "as an artist you can express the same idea in different media", so moving from fine arts to photography, from new media to film work or from making music in an arts context to working as a musician, are not considered unusual.

Others have learned practical skills in larger or more commercial organisations that they feel has helped them with arts jobs. "Working at the BBC taught me about team work, paper work and network constraints", says one. "Work in a travel agency made me more 'professional' in arts work", says another.[15]

Q. 59 What do you consider the main turning points in your career?

Turning points, as might be expected, are highly personal and thus quite difficult to group. For those who are practising primarily as artists, events such as a first solo show, being commissioned, getting gallery representation, getting a dealer, winning a competition, first sale of work or getting Arts Council funding, are all seen as significant turning points.

For others, it is the direct support of other people that marks a turning point: "getting mentoring from an established artist", says one; "other people recognising your potential", says another.

A third group found travel and living in other countries as their primary turning points. One writes simply – "London". Other personal life experiences – such as having a child or being made redundant – represented turning points. For those who moved from non-arts jobs into primarily arts work, a turning point was often experienced when they did something they didn't like.

Gender

Female: 79 per cent
Male: 21 per cent

Answered: 310 out of 508

Age

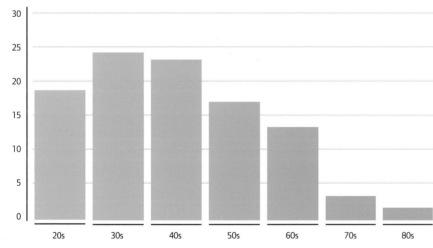

Answered: 310 out of 508

Do you primarily reside in the UK?

Yes: 79 per cent
No: 21 per cent

Answered: 310 out of 508

What is your ethnic group?

White: 78 per cent
Mixed: 3 per cent
Asian: 3 per cent
Black: 1 per cent
Chinese: 2 per cent
Other: 13 per cent

Answered: 309 out of 508

What is your individual gross income from all sources?

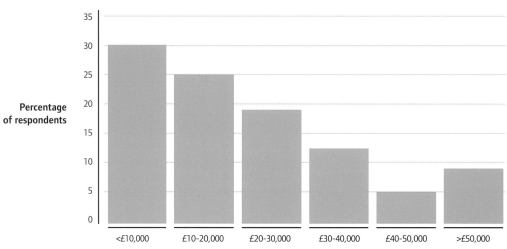

Percentage of respondents

Answered: 306 out of 508

What percentage of your annual income comes from your primary artistic activity?

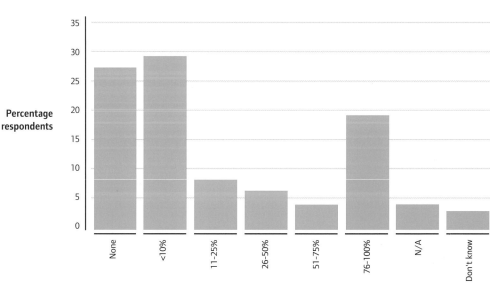

Percentage of respondents

Income levels, as reported above, are relatively low. Although this is consistent with other research on fine artists' incomes (Throsby and Hollister, 2003), it is also likely to be affected by the large numbers of recent graduates in the sample.

Answered: 306 out of 508

Would you be willing to give an interview and participate in further research?

Yes: 67 per cent
No: 33 per cent

Answered: 306 out of 508

Appendix 3: Comparison of main and follow-up survey results

	Original online survey sent to UAL alumni	Abridged survey posted online by Artquest, A-N Newsletter, etc.
Number of Responses	508 responses; 302 completed survey (59%)	115 responses; 93 completed survey (81%)
Where did you study fine arts?	UAL Colleges: 96%	UAL Colleges: 15%
When did you graduate?	1950s: 1% 1960s: 5% 1970s: 9% 1980s: 14% 1990s: 16% 2000s: 54%	1950s: 0% 1960s: 2% 1970s: 6% 1980s: 8% 1990s: 15% 2000s: 70%
Formal training?	Yes: 44%	Yes: 43%
Informal learning?	Yes: 80%	Yes: 93%
Employment status	Employed full-time: 24% Employed part-time: 18% On sabbatical/leave: 1% Self-employed: 40% Unemployed: 6% Retired: 2% Other: 10%	Employed full-time: 12% Employed part-time: 20% On sabbatical/leave: 0% Self-employed: 41% Unemployed: 8% Retired: 2% Other: 18%
Primary occupation (Top 3 answers)	Arts/Cultural Industries: 40% Further/Higher Ed: 14% Other: 9%	Arts/Cultural Industries: 54% Crafts/Applied Art: 8% Further/Higher Ed: 7% Not-for-profit/Charity: 7%
Second job?	Yes: 39%	Yes: 41%
Second job sector (Top 3 answers)	Arts/Cultural Industries: 39% Other: 16% Further/Higher Ed: 12%	Arts/Cultural Industries: 20% Leisure/Hospitality: 17% Other: 17%
Ever a practising artist?	Yes: 87%	Yes: 93%
Primary artistic practice (Top 3 answers)	Painting: 37% Other: 18% Sculpture: 10%	Painting: 32% Other: 18% Sculpture: 15%

	Original online survey sent to UAL alumni		Abridged survey posted online by Artquest, A-N Newsletter, etc.	
Set up a business?	Yes: 45%		Yes: 44%	
Gender	Male: 21%; Female: 79%		Male: 18%; Female: 82%	
Age	80s: 2%		70s: 1%	
	70s: 3%		60s: 8%	
	60s: 13%		50s: 17%	
	50s: 17%		40s: 22%	
	40s: 23%		30s: 17%	
	30s: 24%		20s: 33%	
	20s: 18%			
UK resident	Yes: 79%		Yes: 97%	
Ethnic group	White 79%		White 89%	
	Mixed 3%		Mixed 4%	
	Asian 3%		Asian 1%	
	Black 1%		Black 2%	
	Chinese 2%		Chinese 1%	
	Other 13%		Other 3%	
Gross individual income from all sources	<£10,000	30%	<£10,000	37%
	£10-20,000	25%	£10-19,000	43%
	£20-30,000	19%	£20-29,000	14%
	£30-40,000	13%	£30-39,000	4%
	£40-50,000	5%	£40-49,000	2%
	>£50,000	9%	>£50,000	1%
Percentage of income from primary artistic practice	None	27%	None	22%
	<10%	29%	<10%	33%
	11-25%	8%	11-25%	9%
	26-50%	6%	26-50%	7%
	51-75%	4%	51-75%	10%
	76-100%	19%	76-100%	16%
	N/A	4%	N/A	1%
	Don't Know:	3%	Don't Know:	1%

Appendix 4: Summary of online survey sample characteristics

Sample size

Respondents	508 surveys started
	302 surveys completed (59%)

Demographic Information

Age	20-29: 18% of respondents
	30-39: 24%
	40-49: 23%
	50-59: 17%
	60-69: 13%
	70-79: 3%
	80-89: 2%
Gender	21% Male
	79% Female
Ethnic group	79% White
	3% Mixed
	3% Asian
	1% Black
	2% Chinese
	13% Other
Residency	79% of survey respondents primarily reside in the UK; of those, 70% live in Greater London
Income	30% earn less than £10,000 per year
	25% earn £10-19,000
	19% earn £20-29,000
	13% earn £30-39,000
	5% earn £40-50,000
	9% earn more than £50,000

Education

UAL College(s) attended	Byam Shaw School of Art: 7%
	Camberwell: 15%
	Central Saint Martins: 40%
	Chelsea: 29%
	London College of Communication: 5%

London College of Fashion: 1%
London College of Printing: 4%
Wimbledon: 6%
Other: 4%

Decade of graduation	1% graduated during the 1950s 5% during the 1960s 9% during the 1970s 14% during the 1980s 16% during the 1990s 54% during the 2000s
Level of qualification(s) attained at UAL	BA degree: 39% MA degree: 24% Diploma: 13% Foundation: 5% Other: 5%

Employment

Employment status	24% Employed full-time 18% Employed part-time 1% On leave or sabbatical 40% Self-employed 6% Unemployed 2% Retired 10% Other
Sector of primary occupation	Top 3 sectors 1) Arts and Cultural Industries (40%) 2) Higher, Further, Secondary or Primary Education (20%) 3) Publishing/Media (6%)
Second jobholding	39% of respondents hold a second job
Sector of second job	Top 3 sectors 1) Arts/Cultural Industries (39%) 2) Education (16%) 3) Health care/Medical (8%)
Business start-ups	45% of respondents have set up a business

Artistic Practice

Practising artists	87% of respondents consider (or have considered) themselves to be a practising artist
Primary practice	37% Painting 10% Sculpture 4% Printmaking 7% Photography 2% Digital Arts 7% Film & Video 6% Installation 10% Multi-media 1% None 18% Other
Membership of artists' organisations or studios	64% of respondents are (or have been) members of artists' organisations, studios or collectives

Appendix 5: Table of interview sample

Sample Size

Interviewees	40 in-depth interviews completed

Demographic Information

Age	20-29: 13% of interviewees
	30-39: 30%
	40-49: 25%
	50-59: 15%
	60-69: 15%
	70-79: 3%
Gender	33% Male
	68% Female
Ethnic group	93% White
	8% Asian
Residency	100% of interviewees primarily reside in the UK; of those, 80% live in Greater London
Income	10% earn less than £10,000 per year
	23% earn £10-19,000
	28% earn £20-29,000
	18% earn £30-40,000
	8% earn £40-50,000
	15% earn more than £50,000

Education

UAL College(s) attended	Byam Shaw School of Art: 5%
	Camberwell: 15%
	Central Saint Martins: 65%
	Chelsea: 18%
	London College of Printing: 3%
	Wimbledon: 3%
Decade of graduation	3% graduated during the 1950s
	10% during the 1960s
	18% during the 1970s
	10% during the 1980s

	25% during the 1990s
	33% during the 2000s
Level of qualification(s) attained at UAL	BA degree: 48%
	MA degree: 33%
	Diploma: 23%
	Foundation: 3%
	Other: 5%

Employment

Employment status	40% Employed full-time or part-time
	55% Self-employed
	3% On leave or sabbatical
	3% Retired
Primary occupation	Top 3 sectors
	1) Arts/Cultural Industries (58%)
	2) Other (23%)
	3) Education (20%)
Second jobholding	38% of respondents hold a second job
Sector of second job	Top 3 sectors
	1) Arts/Cultural Industries (40%)
	2) Other (33%)
	3) Education (27%)
Business start-ups	60% of interviewees have set up a business

Artistic Practice

Practising artists	83% of interviewees consider (or have considered) themselves to be a practising artist
Primary practice	30% Painting
	9% Sculpture
	3% Performance
	3% Printmaking
	6% Photography
	6% Film & Video
	15% Installation
	18% Multi-media
	9% Other
Membership of artists' organisations or studios	58% of interviewees are (or have been) members of artists' organisations, studios or collectives

Appendix 6: Bibliography

Andari, R., Bakhshi, H., Hutton, W., O'Keeffe, A. and Schneider, P. (2007) 'Staying ahead, the economic performance of the UK's creative industries.' London: The Work Foundation.

Aston, J. (1999) Ambitions and Destinations: The Careers and Retrospective Views of Art and Design Graduates and Postgraduates. 'International Journal of Art & Design Education.' 18, pp.231-240.

Athey, G., Glossop, C., Harrison, B., Nathan, M. and Webber, C. (2007) 'Innovation and the City.' London: NESTA.

Bain, A. (2005) Constructing an Artistic Identity. 'Work, Employment and Society.' 19 (1), pp.25-46.

Bakhshi, H., McVittie, E. and Simmie, J. (2008) 'Creating Innovation: do the creative industries stimulate innovation in the wider economy.' London: NESTA.

Bathelt, H., Malmberg, A. and Maskell, P. (2004) Clusters and Knowledge: Local Buzz, Global Pipelines and the Process of Knowledge Creation. 'Progress in Human Geography.' 28, pp.31-56.

Becker, G. (1964) 'Human Capital: A Theoretical and Empirical Analysis, with Special Reference to Education.' Chicago: University of Chicago Press.

Becker, H. (1982) 'Art Worlds.' Berkeley: University of California Press.

Bell, D. (1976) 'The Cultural Contradictions of Capitalism.' New York: Basic Books.

Benhamou, F. (2002) Artists' labour markets. In Towse, R. (ed.) 'A Handbook of Cultural Economics.' Cheltenham: Edward Elgar.

Bilton, C. (2007) 'Management and Creativity.' Oxford: Blackwell Publishing.

Bird, E. (2000) 'Art and Design Education: Historical Overview.' Working Papers in Art and Design 1. Hatfield: University of Hertfordshire.

Blackwell, B. and Harvey, D. (1999) 'Destinations and Reflections: Careers of British Art, Craft and Design Graduates.' Birmingham: Centre for Research into Quality, UCE.

Boltanski, L. and Chiapello, E. (2005) 'The New Spirit of Capitalism.' London: Verso.

Bourdieu, P. (1984) 'Distinction: a Social Critique of the Judgement of Taste.' London: Routledge & Kegan Paul.

Bracewell, M. (2007) 'Remake/Re-model: Art, Pop, Fashion and the making of Roxy Music.' London: Faber and Faber.

Bryce, J., Mendelovits, J., Beavis, A., McQueen, J. and Adams, I. (2004) 'Evaluation of School-based Arts Education Programmes in Australian Schools.' Camberwell: Australian Council for Educational Research.

Bunting, C. (2007) 'Public value and the arts in England: Discussion and conclusions of the arts debate.' London: Arts Council England.

Burton, J., Horowitz, R. and Abeles, H. (2000) Learning in and through the arts: The question of transfer. 'Studies in Art Education.' 41(3), pp.228-257.

Castañer, X. and Campos, L. (2002) The Determinants of Artistic Innovation: Bringing in the role of organisations. 'Journal of Cultural Economics.' 26, pp.29-52.

Caves, R. (2000) 'Creative Industries: Contracts between arts and commerce.' Cambridge, MA: Harvard University Press.

Charmaz, K. (2006) 'Constructing Grounded Theory.' London: Sage Publications.

Cunningham, S. (2006) 'What Price a Creative Economy?' Sydney: Platform Papers.

Currid, E. (2007) 'The Warhol Economy: How Fashion, Art, and Music Drive New York City.' Princeton: University Press.

DCMS (2008) 'Creative Britain: New Talents for the New Economy.' London: DCMS.

Davies, R. and Lindley, R.M. (2003) 'Artists in Figures: A Statistical Portrait of Cultural Occupations.' London: Arts Council of England.

Dodgson, M., Gann, D. and Salter, A. (2005) 'Think, Play, Do: technology, innovation and organisation.' Oxford: Oxford University Press.

Florida, R. (2002) 'The Rise of the Creative Class.' New York: Basic Books.

Frey, B.S. (1997, 2000 2nd ed.) 'Not Just for the Money: an Economic Theory of Personal Motivation.' Cheltenham: Edward Elgar.

Frey, B.S. and Pommerehne, W.W. (1989) 'Muses and Markets: Explorations in the Economics of the Arts.' Oxford: Basil Blackwell.

Frith, S. and Horne, H. (1987) 'Art Into Pop.' London: Methuen.

Gill, R. (2007) 'Techobohemians or the new Cybertariat? New media work in Amsterdam a decade after the Web.' Amsterdam: Institute of Network Cultures.

Gilmore, S. (1988) Schools of Activity and Innovation. 'The Sociological Quarterly.' 29, pp.203-219.

Halfacree, K. and Boyle, P. (1993) The challenge facing biographical research; the case for a biographical approach. 'Progress in Human Geography.' 17, pp.333-348.

Harvey, D. and Blackwell, B. (1999) Gender Bias in Incomes of UK Art and Design Graduates. 'Industry and Higher Education.' 13, pp.323-29.

Heath, J. and Potter, A. (2005) 'The Rebel Sell: How the counterculture became consumer culture.' Chichester, West Sussex: Capstone Publishing.

Heinz, W. and Kruger, H. (2001) Life Course: Innovations and Challenges for Social Research. 'Current Sociology.' March 2001, Vol. 49 (2), pp.29-45.

HESA (2005) 'Annual Statistics, Table 2e - all HE students by level of study, mode of study, subject of study (#1), domicile and gender 2005/06.' Retrieved 24 January 2008 from: http://www.hesa.ac.uk/dox/ dataTables/studentsAndQualifiers/download/subject0506.xls

Hesmondhalgh, D. (2002) 'The Cultural Industries.' London: Sage.

Higgs, P., Cunningham, S. and Bakhshi, H. (2008) 'Beyond the Creative Industries: Mapping the Creative Economy in the United Kingdom.' London: NESTA.

HM Treasury (2005) 'Cox Review of Creativity in Business.' London: HM Treasury.

Jarvis, H. and Pratt, A.C. (2006) Bringing it all back home: the extensification and 'overflowing' of work. The case of San Francisco's new media households. 'Geoforum.' 37, pp.331-339.

KEA (2006) 'The Economy of Culture in Europe': KEA European Affairs

Knell, J. and Oakley, K. (2007) 'London's Creative Economy: An Accidental Success.' London: The Work Foundation.

Knudsen, B., Florida, R. and Stolarick, K. (forthcoming) Beyond Spillovers: The Effects of Creative Density on Innovation. Forthcoming in 'Annals of the Association of American Geographers.'

Lampert, N. (2006) Critical Thinking Dispositions as an outcome of arts education. 'Studies in Art Education.' Vol. 47, No. 3, Spring.

Lash, S. and Urry, C. (1993) 'Economies of signs and space.' London: Sage Publications.

Lash, S. and Urry, C. (2007) 'Global Cultural Industry.' Cambridge: Polity.

Latour, B. (1988) 'The Pasteurization of France.' Cambridge, MA: Harvard University Press.

Leadbeater, C. (1999) 'Living on Thin Air.' London: Penguin.

Leadbeater, C. and Oakley, K. (1999) 'The Independents.' London: Demos.

Lester, R. and Piore, M. (2004) 'Innovation: The Missing Dimension.' Cambridge, MA: Harvard University Press.

Lloyd, R. (2006) 'Neo-Bohemia, Arts and Commerce in the post-industrial city.' New York: Routledge.

MacDonald, S. (2005) 'A Century of Arts and Design Education.' Cambridge: Lutterworth Press.

Markusen, A. and King, H. (2003) 'The Artistic Dividend: The Arts Hidden Contribution to Regional Development.' Available at: www.hhh.umn.edu/projects/prie/pub.htm

Markusen, A., Gilmore, S., Johnson, A., Levi, T. and Martinez, A. (2006) 'Crossover: How Artists Build Careers across Commercial, Nonprofit, Community Work.' Minneapolis: Hubert Humphrey Institute of Public Affairs, University of Minnesota.

McRobbie, A. (2000) From Clubs to Companies. 'Zwischen Forum and Basar Forum Stadpark.' File 1, 2000, pp.43-57.

McRobbie, A. (2002) From Holloway to Hollywood: happiness at work in the new cultural economy? In Du Gay and Pryke (eds, 2002) 'Cultural Economy.' London: Sage.

Menger, P. (1999) Artistic labor markets and careers. 'Annual Review Sociology.' 25, pp.541-74.

Miles, I. and Green, L. (2008) 'Hidden Innovation in the Creative Industries.' London: NESTA.

Ministry of Education (1960) 'First Report of the National Advisory Council on Art Education.' London: Ministry of Education.

Mommaas, H. (2004) Cultural Clusters and the Post-Industrial City, towards the remapping of urban cultural policy. 'Urban Studies.' 41(3), pp.507-32.

Mulvey, J. (2006) 'Inside HE: Art of Freedom.' Newcastle-upon-Tyne: HERO.

Neff, G. (2005) The Changing Place of Cultural production: The Location of Social Networks in a digital media industry. 'The Annals of the American Academy of Political and Social Science.' Vol. 597, No. 1, pp.134-152.

NESTA (2006a) 'The Innovation Gap: Why policy needs to reflect the reality of innovation in the UK.' London: NESTA.

NESTA (2006b) 'Creating Growth: How the UK can develop world-class creative businesses.' London: NESTA.

NESTA (2007) 'How linked at the UK's creative industries to the wider economy?' NESTA Working Paper. London: NESTA.

Nonaka, I. (1991) The Knowledge Creating Company. 'Harvard Business Review.' November-December, 1001.

Nonaka, I. and Takeuchi, H. (1995) 'The knowledge creating company.' Oxford: Oxford University Press.

Oakley, K. and Sperry, B. (2008) 'Fine artists and innovation – a longitudinal study on the impact of fine artists on the UK economy.' NESTA Working Paper. London: NESTA.

Oakley, K. (2006) Include us out – economic development and social policy in the creative industries. 'Cultural Trends.' Vol. 14, No. 4, pp.283-302.

Pratt, A. (2000) New media, the new economy and new spaces. 'Geoforum.' 31, pp.425-436.

Pratt, A. (2002) Hot jobs in cool places: The material cultures of new media product spaces; the case of the South of the Market, San Francisco. 'Information, Communication and Society.' 5/1, pp.27-50.

Pratt, A. (2005a) 'New media: work organisation and place.' Paper presented at the International Labour Process Conference, University of Strathclyde.

Pratt, A. (2005b) 'Digitisation and face to face interactions: the example of the film industry in London.' Unpublished.

Pratt, A. (2006) Advertising and creativity, a governance approach: a case study of creative agencies in London. 'Environment and Planning.' A 38, pp.1883–1899.

Randle, K. and Culkin, N. (2007) 'Getting in and getting on in Hollywood: Freelance careers in an uncertain industry.' Paper presented at the Expert Seminar on Precarious Labour in the E Society, LSE, March 2007.

Rengers, M. and Madden, C. (2000) Living Art: Artists Between Making Art and Making a Living. 'Australian Bulletin of Labour.' 26, pp.325-54.

Rogers, E. (2003) 'Diffusion of Innovations.' New York: Simon and Schuster.

Ross, A. (2003) 'No Collar: The humane workplace and its hidden costs.' Philadelphia: Temple University Press.

Scott, A.J. (2000) 'The Cultural Economy of Cities.' London: Sage.

Seltzer, K. and Bentley, T. (1999) 'The Creative Age.' London: Demos.

Stoneman, P. (2007) 'An Introduction to the Definition and Measurement of Soft Innovation.' NESTA Working Paper. London: NESTA.

Stoneman, P. (2008) 'Soft innovation in creative and non creative industries.' NESTA Working Paper. London: NESTA.

Storper, M. and Venables, A.J. (2004) Buzz: face-to-face contact and the urban economy. 'Journal of Economic Geography.' 4, pp.351-370.

Taylor, S. and Littleton, K. (2008) Art work or money: conflicts in the construction of a creative identity. 'Sociological Review.' 56:2, pp.275-292.

Throsby, D. (1992) Artists as workers. In Towse and Khakee (eds) 'Cultural Economics.' Heidelberg: Springer.

Throsby, D. (1994) A Work-Preference Model of Artist Behaviour. In Peacock and Rizzo (eds) 'Cultural Economics and Cultural Policies.' Boston: Kluwer.

Throsby, D. (2001) Defining the Artistic Workforce: The Australian Experience. 'Poetics.' 28, pp.255-271.

Throsby, D. (2001) 'Economics and Culture.' Cambridge: Cambridge University Press.

Throsby, D. (2006) An Artistic Production Function: Theory and an Application to Australian Visual Artists. 'Journal of Cultural Economics.' 30, pp.1-14.

Throsby, D. and Hollister, H. (2003) 'Don't Give Up your day job: an economic study of professional artists in Australia.' Sydney: Australia Council.

Throsby, D. and Mills, D. (1989) 'When Are you Going to Get a Real Job?' Sydney: Australia Council.

Throsby, D. and Thompson, B. (1994) 'But What Do You Do for a Living? A New Economic Study of Australian Artists.' Sydney: Australia Council.

Timms, B. and Wright, S. (2007) 'So what do you do?' London: Demos.

Towse, R. (1992) 'Economic and Social Characteristics of Artists in Wales.' Cardiff: Welsh Arts Council.

Towse, R. (1995) 'Economic of Artist's Labour Markets.' London: Arts Council of England.

Towse, R. (1996) Economics of Training Artists. In Ginsberg and Menger (eds) 'Economics of the Arts, Selected Essays.' Amsterdam: Elsevier.

Towse, R. (2001) Partly for the Money: Rewards and Incentives to Artists. 'Kyklos.' 54, 2/3, pp.473-490.

Towse, R. (2004) 'Towards an Economics of Creativity?' Paper presented at the FOKUS Vienna Workshop on Creative Industries. Available at: http://www.recida.org/

Verganti, R. (2003) Design as Brokering of Languages: The Role of Designers in the Innovation Strategies of Italian Firms. 'Design Management Journal.' 3, pp.34-42.

Wenger, E. (1998) 'Communities of Practice.' Cambridge: Cambridge University Press.

Williams, R. (1976) 'Keywords.' London: Fontana.